A gift for:

_____

From:

_____

the Beauty of GOD'S BLESSINGS

DAILY INSPIRATION FOR WOMEN

In quietness and confidence

shall be your strength.

Isaiah 30:15

January

*I want what God wants,
that's why I am so merry.*

—St. Francis of Assisi

God is interested in the texture of our days. One thing I've come to accept is that some days are busier than others; if we choose to participate in life, we cannot avoid this ebb and flow. On the flow days, when urgency drives us and we lurch (late) from one event to the next, we can pray for time . . . and God will give us little corners to cut so we don't have to be so breathless.

LESLIE WILLIAMS
Seduction of the Lesser Gods

༉

*The LORD has done great things for us,
and we are glad.*

PSALM 126:3

The word *impossible* melts away with God. He knows no defeat; can turn every failure and frustration into unexpected victory. He can reverse a doctor's grim prognosis. With Him a seemingly dark and desolate future becomes a joyous new life.

CATHERINE MARSHALL
Moments that Matter

With God all things are possible.
MATTHEW 19:26

13

The mustard seed is one of the smallest seeds in the world. It takes very little faith to grow big miracles. But sometimes I find having even the smallest amount of faith the most difficult thing in the world—especially when times are hard.

Hebrews 11:1 . . . tells us to cultivate faith the size of a very tiny seed and let it grow in the ground of our own pain. Such faith, sown in pain, is a miracle great enough to move mountains.

HARRIET CROSBY
A Well-Watered Garden

⟩⟩

Now faith is the substance of things hoped for, the evidence of things not seen.

HEBREWS 11:1

Christ has already given us everything when He gave us Himself. He asks for everything in return—there must be no reserved corners, no secret disclaimers, no insistence on individual rights, no escape clauses.

Obedience is part of love's burden.

ELISABETH ELLIOT
The Path of Loneliness

❧

We love Him because He first loved us.
1 JOHN 4:19

15

The best of blessings do not always come in crowds.

There are those still, quiet moments when alone in gentle communion with Christ I sense and see the momentary glory of His person. The intense nearness of His Spirit as soft, yet sublime moves on my spirit. And again I know, "O Father, You are here!"

W. PHILLIP KELLER
Sea Edge

☙

The LORD is my strength and song,
and He has become my salvation.
PSALM 118:14

The Kiga tribe in East Africa gives God the name of Biheko, which means "a God who carries everyone on His back." In this tribe, only mothers and older sisters carry children on their backs. To portray Biheko, one of their artists made a wooden carving of a man carrying on his back a child with an adult face and in his arms a weaker child. This carving is a symbol of the God who takes care of human beings with the tender care of a mother.

INGRID TROBISCH
The Confident Woman

ॐ

*I have made you
and I will carry you.*
ISAIAH 46:4, NIV

17

The most interesting people I know drink in life and savor every drop—the sweet and the sour. The good and the bad. The planned and the unplanned. And isn't that what God intends? When Jesus modeled humanity for you and me to see, He was out there—everywhere! He took risks. He embraced life and responded to everyone and everything, the tender and the tumultuous. His capacity for life was without measure. And we are designed like Him. Fully human and fully alive.

LUCI SWINDOLL
I Married Adventure

ᔜ

*Nothing is better for them than
to rejoice, and to do good in their lives.*
ECCLESIASTES 3:12

The more time we spend praising the Lord,
the more we will see ourselves and our
circumstances grow in wholeness and
completeness. That's because praise softens
our hearts and makes them pliable. It also
covers us protectively. The more the pliability
and covering are maintained, the more quickly
our hearts can be molded and healed.

STORMIE OMARTIAN
Praying God's Will for Your Life

❧

Sing praise to the LORD,…
and give thanks at the
remembrance of His holy name.
PSALM 30:4

Prayer is a way for us to connect with God's plan. It is not about figuring a way to get God into our plan....

Lay down your market lists of wants. Lay down your teaspoon. Then go, through prayer, to the well of God's love with the biggest container you can find.

SUZANNE DALE EZELL
Living Again in God's Abundance

༜

To You, O LORD, I lift up my soul.
O my God, I trust in You.
PSALM 25:1–2

Frequently people say to me, "God answered my prayer!" Usually they mean God granted them whatever they had requested, either for themselves or for others.

God *always* answers the prayers of His children—but His answer isn't always "Yes." Sometimes His answer is "No," or "Wait"— and they are answers just as much as "Yes."

BILLY GRAHAM
Unto the Hills

Let us . . . come boldly to the throne
of grace, that we may obtain mercy.

HEBREWS 4:16

21

We are only finite human beings. We can only see the present and the past. The future is a little frightening to us. So we need to hold onto God's hand and trust Him to calm our fears.

CHARLES SWINDOLL
The Mystery of God's Will

Stand fast in the Lord.
PHILIPPIANS 4:1

The family of God is a large and rather odd bunch. Some folks we like. Others we like a little less. But out of respect for our Father God, we call each other brother and sister and know that the same grace we extend to others, others also are extending to us.

ALICIA BRITT CHOLE
Pure Joy

❧

*Let us not give up meeting together, . . .
but let us encourage one another.*
HEBREWS 10:25, NIV

God has been making arrangements for your part in His plan long before you were born. He is never unprepared. Your past does not surprise Him. Your present does not worry Him. Your future is not a mystery to Him. No one is a second-class laborer in His harvest. You are precious to Him. He is The Almighty, you are His beloved child, and we are all part of the wonderful tapestry of His eternal purposes.

ALICIA BRITT CHOLE
Pure Joy

*I will praise you, LORD, with all my heart
and tell about the wonders you have worked.*
PSALM 9:1, CEV

I n His death Jesus Christ gave us life. The willingness of the Son of God to commit Himself into the hands of criminals became the greatest gift ever given—the Bread of the world, in mercy broken. Thus the worst thing that ever happened became the best that ever happened.

ELISABETH ELLIOT
The Path of Loneliness

The wages of sin is death, but the gift of God is eternal life in Christ Jesus our Lord.

ROMANS 6:23

The power in your life and mine that results in blessings is in direct proportion to the extent that you are willing to die to your own will, your own goals, your own dreams, your own desires, your own wants, your own plans, your own rights, your own reputation. It's what Jesus meant when He challenged His disciples, "If anyone would come after me, he must deny himself and take up his cross and follow me."

ANNE GRAHAM LOTZ
My Heart's Cry

‍‍‍‍‍‍‍‍‍‍‍‍‍‍‍‍‍‍‍‍‍‍‍‍‍‍‍‍ک

*If anyone would come after me, he must deny
himself and take up his cross and follow me.*
MATTHEW 16:24 NIV

Heaven will be a spacious place, and all sorts of treasures will be available to us there. But the entryway is too small for a moving van; we can't take anything with us to paradise except the love we carry inside our hearts.

BARBARA JOHNSON
He's Gonna Toot

∾

What does the LORD require of you
but to do justly, to love mercy,
and to walk humbly with your God?
MICAH 6:8

27

God will keep us. He'll help. He'll intervene—perhaps just in the nick of time. Is that too close for comfort? Maybe. But our trust in Him was never meant to be comfortable—only close. And the nick of time is close enough.

JONI EARECKSON TADA
Holiness in Hidden Places

༽

Certainly God has heard me;
He has attended to the voice of my prayer.

PSALM 66:19

Isn't it good to know that even when we don't love with a perfect love, God does? He always nourishes what is right. He always applauds what is right. He has never done wrong, led one person to do wrong, or rejoiced when anyone did wrong. For He is love, and love "does not rejoice in unrighteousness, but rejoices with the truth."

MAX LUCADO
A Love Worth Giving

⸙

[Love] does not rejoice in unrighteousness,
but rejoices with the truth.

1 CORINTHIANS. 13:6, NASB

Why do we expect ease as our due? The Bible is filled with people who struggled, and many who died for their faith. Jesus Himself said that our lives as Christians would be difficult. God fills our lives with challenges, not bonbons, because it is the challenges that bring us closer to Him and ultimately bring us joy.

LESLIE WILLIAMS
Seduction of the Lesser Gods

≈

Refrain your voice from weeping,
and your eyes from tears;
for your work shall be rewarded.

JEREMIAH 31:16

J esus is big enough to do the things you have labeled impossible. He has enough power. He has enough time. He is bigger than your problem.

Believe in Him more than in what you may see. Trust in Him more than what you may feel. God is highly confident of His own plans. He can do everything but fail.

KATHY TROCCOLI
Hope for a Woman's Heart

∾

Great is the LORD,
and greatly to be praised.
PSALM 48:1

G od wants your fellowship, and He has done everything possible to make it a reality. He has forgiven your sins, at the cost of His own dear Son. He has given you His Word, and the priceless privilege of prayer and worship.

He will come near to you, if you will come near to Him.

BILLY GRAHAM
Unto the Hills

❧

Come near to God and
he will come near to you.

JAMES 4:8, NIV

I must be faithful to provide the conditions for growth in my spiritual garden by practicing the disciplines of prayer, Bible study, and worship. But it is God who brings about deep, lasting spiritual growth. And that takes a lifetime. . . . God grows my spirit in His own time, and because He takes the long view, so can I. That is the joy of grace.

HARRIET CROSBY
A Well-Watered Garden

God gave the growth.

1 CORINTHIANS 3:6, NRSV

33

When we allow the Spirit to guide us He will concern Himself with our every desire and need—how we use our time and spend our money. With honesty and moral integrity and Christ-like quality of character; with what is happening to our children; with the health of our relationships with other people and with God. And, if our need is severe enough, the Holy Spirit will turn our lives upside down.

CATHERINE MARSHALL
Moments that Matter

ა

We all . . . are being transformed into the same image . . . by the Spirit of the Lord.

2 CORINTHIANS 3:18

How unbelievably awesome is the One Who created everything!

Our heads should bow, our knees should bend, our wills should yield, our hands should serve, our minds should worship, and our hearts should love the One Whose glory is revealed in the beginning through His eternity, deity, activity, and identity.

ANNE GRAHAM LOTZ
God's Story

ॐ

*In the beginning God created
the heavens and the earth.*
GENESIS 1:1

January 25

When we watch what we say we reap
the benefit of protection from
adversity, affliction, hardship, and misery.
Keeping your mouth is keeping yourself.
Through patience or calmness and
composure, the rulers in your life can be
influenced. Gentle words can break the
toughest structure of anyone. They melt
away hardness.

LISA BEVERE
Be Angry but Don't Blow It!

୬

Watch your words and hold your tongue;
you'll save yourself a lot of grief.
PROVERBS 21:23, *THE MESSAGE*

Picture mature gnarled trees. Their limbs wide and thick with leaves and loaded with fruit. Standing strong by a stream rushing with life, water spilling and splashing over the rocks. They're strong, firm, confident, and fruitful.

People who delight in God's Word and His will are like those trees. The source of the fruitfulness is a living, active relationship with God and His Word.

PETER WALLACE
What the Psalmist Is Saying

＊

They are like trees growing beside a stream,
trees that produce fruit
in season and always have leaves.

PSALM 1:3, CEV

When will we ever learn that there are no hopeless situations, only people who have grown hopeless about them? What appears as an unsolvable problem to us is actually a rather exhilarating challenge. People who inspire others are those who see invisible bridges at the end of dead-end streets.

CHARLES SWINDOLL
Dropping Your Guard

꿍

Let this mind be in you which
was also in Christ Jesus.

PHILIPPIANS 2:5

God has proven Himself a faithful Father. Now it falls to us to be trusting children. Let God give you what your family doesn't. Let Him fill the void others have left. Rely upon Him for your affirmation and encouragement.

MAX LUCADO
He Still Moves Stones

❧

You are God's child, and God will give you the blessing he promised, because you are his child.

GALATIANS 4:7, NCV

Every day God reminds us to quit holding things too tightly—whether an event, a viewpoint, a desire, a particular time in life, or a person we thoroughly enjoy. He urges us to stop struggling, resisting, coercing, or manipulating for what we want. When we simply do what He asks, no matter how hard it seems, and we keep our focus on the Light of the world, an amazing brightness comes, all within the embrace of His love.

LUCI SWINDOLL
I Married Adventure

❧

My soul, wait silently for God alone,
for my expectation is from Him.

PSALM 62:5

God's peace doesn't guarantee we won't be touched by the world. No. Jesus assured us we *will* be knocked around by evils the world inflicts on its inhabitants. Rather, God's peace is like an inner lining to keep the world's fears and destruction from eating and destroying our souls.

LESLIE WILLIAMS
Night Wrestling

*God is the strength of my heart
and my portion forever.*
PSALM 73:26

A journalist visiting a jungle mission outpost said to a nurse who was caring for a patient, "It must be difficult to be buried out here."

As she cleansed the patient's ugly wound, the nurse smiled and replied, "I wasn't buried. I was planted."

WARREN W. WIERSBE
The 20 Essential Qualities

᠄

The fruit of the righteous is a tree of life.
PROVERBS 11:30

February

Heaven will be the perfection
we have always longed for.
—BILLY GRAHAM

Remember Jesus in the Garden of Gethsemane? He dreaded what was to come to pass and prayed for deliverance. His, prayer, however, was not the petulant demand of an angry child, but the humble petition of an obedient son: *Father, if You are willing.* Jesus did not want anything contrary to what His Father wanted. The "cup" was not removed. Escape was not granted. The second part of the prayer was granted: *Your will be done.*

ELISABETH ELLIOT
The Music of His Promises

❧

I trust in Your word.
PSALM 119:42

A friend is someone to whom I do not have to explain myself. Such a friendship offers unspeakable comfort. . . .

In some friendships, we must do more giving. It is then that we are called to become midwives for whatever God is bringing to birth in our friends. In other friendships, we are more on the receiving end. It is important to balance our friendships so that sometimes we are the givers and other times we are the receivers.

INGRID TROBISCH
The Confident Woman

෯

I have called you friends.
JOHN 15:15

A mother bird is a fascinating creature, capable of warm, careful concern, on the one hand, and fierce protective defense of her children, on the other.

And in that illustration you can catch a glimpse of God's care for you. God covers you with His wings so you are warm and protected from the elements. You are able to grow as you should. All your needs are provided. And you can nest in His love.

PETER WALLACE
What the Psalmist Is Saying

෨

He will spread his wings over you
and keep you secure.

PSALM 91:4, CEV

It was Jesus' custom to rise before dawn and slip outdoors to pray. A hillside or lakeside was His favorite spot for teaching. (Matt. 13:1–2) A boat pushed out from the shore made a perfect pulpit. (Mark 4:1) An olive grove in the Garden of Gethsemane was a favorite spot.

We, too, need to slip away to be refreshed in the quietness and beauty of God's great outdoors.

CATHERINE MARSHALL
Moments that Matter

To You, O LORD,
I lift up my soul.
PSALM 25:1

47

Worry makes you feel worthless, forgotten, and unimportant. That's why Jesus says that we are worth much more than the birds of the air who neither worry nor die of hunger because their heavenly Father feeds them. They enjoy what's there. If God is able to sustain the lesser creatures, won't He sustain the greater?

CHARLES SWINDOLL
Perfect Trust

༄

Look at the birds of the air, for they
neither sow nor reap . . . yet
your heavenly Father feeds them.
MATTHEW 6:26

People are much like freshly fallen snow. As we interact with each other we leave impressions in each other's souls. As we walk together, we leave footprints in each other's paths. As family or friends, we leave traces of ourselves in each other's minds and hearts.

What kind of traces do we leave?

ALICIA BRITT CHOLE
Pure Joy

꙳

Blessed are the pure in heart,
for they shall see God.

MATTHEW 5:8

49

Those who submit to the will of God do not fight back at life. They learn the secret of yielding—of relinquishing and abandoning—their own lives and wills to Christ. And then He gives back to them a life that is far richer and fuller than anything they could ever have imagined.

BILLY GRAHAM
Unto the Hills

*[She] who loses [her] life
for My sake shall find it.*
MATTHEW 10:39

D o you ever feel unnoticed? New clothes and styles may help for a while. But if you want permanent change, learn to see yourself as God sees you: "He has covered me with clothes of salvation and wrapped me with a coat of goodness, like a bridegroom dressed for his wedding, like a bride dressed in jewels" (Isa. 61:10, NCV).

Allow God's love to change the way you look at you.

MAX LUCADO
When Christ Comes

☙

You are . . . God's own possession.
1 PETER 2:9, NCV

February 9

I love to think of the preparations God is making for my homecoming one day. He knows the colors I love, the scenery I enjoy, the things that make me happy. All these personal details will let me know when I walk into My Father's House, that I am expected and welcome because He has prepared it for me! And in the same way, He is preparing a glorious homecoming for *you!*

ANNE GRAHAM LOTZ
Heaven: My Father's House

౨

*Rejoice because your names
are written in heaven.*

LUKE 10:20

52

God is eternal, infinite, sovereign, omnipotent, omniscient, omnipresent, and immutable. In addition, He is perfect love, grace, patience and compassion. He's holy, righteous, just, and faithful. God is all of these things every day, all the time, and I count on it because it says so in the Bible, and I believe the Bible to be absolutely true.

LUCI SWINDOLL
I Married Adventure

✧

Behold, God is exalted by His power.
JOB 36:22

To know God is to love God.
To love God is to serve God.
To know Him better is to love Him more.
To love Him more is to serve Him even more . . . as increasingly we line up with His unique plan and purpose for our lives.

ANNE GRAHAM LOTZ
My Heart's Cry

ى

We are His worksmanship,
created in Christ Jesus for good works.
EPHESIANS 2:10

Oswald Chambers said that instead of contradicting God's presence, clouds are actually "a sign that He is there." They are "the dust of our Father's feet," he wrote. Now *that's* an image that makes me smile— God kicking up dust as He strides across the skies! And the thought that we'll someday be soaring upward, blasting right through those "dust clouds" on our way to heaven, certainly brings laughter to my heart.

BARBARA JOHNSON
He's Gonna Toot

*You make the outgoings
of the morning and evening rejoice.*

PSALM 65:8

Labels, labels, labels. I'm glad Jesus referred to people as people. He never mentioned His friend being a coward, He simply called him Peter. He never referred to the woman who loved Him deeply as a prostitute, He just called her Mary Magdalene.

JONI EARECKSON TADA
Holiness in Hidden Places

~

The LORD is merciful and gracious,
slow to anger, and abounding in mercy.
PSALM 103:8

God loves you. Personally. Powerfully. Passionately. Others have promised and failed. But God has promised and succeeded. He loves you with an unfailing love. And His love—if you will let it—can fill you and leave you with a love worth giving.

MAX LUCADO
A Love Worth Giving

ॐ

God is love.
1 JOHN 4:8

57

Undergirding each of the choices we make in life, God is leading us. In our ignorance or in our false desires, we may make what we think is the "wrong" choice; however, because of God's redemption on the cross, there are no ultimate "wrong" choices. God redeems all our blunders, all our stupidity. The crucial choice is choosing God over not choosing God.

LESLIE WILLIAMS
Night Wrestling

ॐ

*The LORD went before them by day
in a pillar of cloud to lead the way, and
by night in a pillar of fire to give them light.*

EXODUS 13:21

Daily, in a discipline of total obedience to God's will and wishes, my old, selfish life must be crossed out in conformity to His character.

It is the result of deliberate surrender of my will to His wishes with glad abandon. It is what happens when I allow the fullness of His wondrous life to sweep over me as the sea sweeps over the shore.

W. PHILLIP KELLER
Sea Edge

༈

He satisfies the longing soul,
and fills the hungry
soul with goodness.

PSALM 107:9

59

H appy are the meek. Happy are the yielded. Happy are those who trustingly put their lives, their fortunes, and their futures in the capable hands of their Creator. Happy are those who "let go and let God."

BILLY GRAHAM
The Secret of Happiness

↭

*Say to the righteous that
it shall be well with them.*

ISAIAH 3:10

We make the mistake of thinking that service to others has to involve some stupendous deed or dramatic sacrifice. Jesus clearly taught us otherwise.

Once or twice in a lifetime, we may have an opportunity to perform the extraordinary deed; but opportunities to do ordinary deeds in extraordinary ways come to us almost daily.

WARREN W. WIERSBE
The 20 Essential Qualities

~

Be especially careful when you are
trying to be good so that
you don't make a performance out of it.
MATTHEW 6:1, *THE MESSAGE*

G od's Book is a veritable storehouse of
promises—over seven thousand of
them. Not empty hopes and dreams, not just
nice-sounding, eloquently worded thoughts
that make you feel warm all over, but
promises. Verbal guarantees in writing,
signed by the Creator Himself.

CHARLES SWINDOLL
The Finishing Touch

❧

I am the way, the truth, and the life.
JOHN 14:6

The measure we use on others is the measure that will be used on us. This is the order of the law. . . . People who execute judgment without mercy reap judgment without mercy. Most of us are not members of the judicial system, yet every day we participate in it to one degree or another. It is found in our actions and our speech.

LISA BEVERE
Be Angry but Don't Blow It!

❧

Mercy triumphs over judgment!
JAMES 2:13, *NIV*

When we're creative, God enjoys the labors of our hands. When we give of ourselves and our possessions, He applauds. When we're merciful, extending grace and forgiveness to those who have hurt us, He cheers. And when we do right, standing up for His will and way, He absolutely loves it!

PETER WALLACE
What the Psalmist Is Saying

⌘

The LORD always does right and wants justice done. Everyone who does right will see his face.

PSALM 11:7, CEV

In *The Lion, the Witch, and the Wardrobe,* Lucy says of Aslan, the lion and Christ figure in the story, "He isn't safe; but he is good." When we trust our worries, ourselves, and our loved ones to the living God of the universe . . . we let God have His way over uncontrollable situations and people. The outcome is not ours to produce but God's to direct. A particular outcome may or may not be what we want. God is not safe. But God is good.

HARRIET CROSBY
A Place Called Home

᪣

*He is a shield to those
who put their trust in Him.*

PROVERBS 30:5

With what misgivings we turn over our lives to God, imagining somehow that we are about to lose everything that matters. Our hesitancy is like that of a tiny shell on the seashore, afraid to give up the teaspoonful of water it holds lest there not be enough ocean to fill it up again. Lose your life, said Jesus, and you will find it. Give up, and I will give you all.

ELISABETH ELLIOT
The Path of Loneliness

ॐ

Whoever loses his life
for My sake will find it.
MATTHEW 16:25

True worship centers on Jesus. It is not about us. It is about Him. It has *always* been about Him and nothing else. It is not about the arts, culture, tradition. It is not about style. It is not about musical preference. Worship is not even about music, period. It's not about anything but *Him.*

FAWN PARISH
It's All About You, Jesus

ॐ

I will . . . praise Your name
for Your lovingkindness and Your truth.

PSALM 138:2

Y ou have not been sprinkled with forgiveness. You have not been spattered with grace. You have not been dusted with kindness. You have been immersed in it. You are submerged in mercy. You are a minnow in the ocean of God's mercy. Let it change you!

MAX LUCADO
A Love Worth Giving

❧

*For You, LORD, are good, and ready
to forgive, and abundant
in mercy to all those who call upon You.*

PSALM 86:5

When a child behaves badly, the child's mother loves him just the same. She may be grieved, disappointed, and hurt, but nothing the child can do will ever destroy her love. If that is true of imperfect human love, how much more so God's love!

It is God's nature to love us. Nothing we can do or fail to do can stop the shining of that great love.

CATHERINE MARSHALL
Moments that Matter

The LORD is good;
His mercy is everlasting.
PSALM 100:5

February 27

God made us, and He wants us to rejoice in our being. Delighting in our personhood is not the same as inflating our egos. Big egos are a result of fluffing ourselves out of insecurity. When we live in gratitude for our won lives and our gifts, then and only then can we freely love others.

LESLIE WILLIAMS
Seduction of the Lesser Gods

ॐ

I will praise You, for I am
fearfully and wonderfully made.

PSALM 139:14

Without knowing God and knowing who we are in Him, we will constantly take our faith on a roller-coaster ride. It will go up and it will go down. We'll scream at the treacherous turns and close our eyes when we start speeding into a steep downward spiral. Trust doesn't change God, but it will certainly change the ride.

KATHY TROCCOLI
Hope for a Woman's Heart

⌒

*The LORD will accomplish
what concerns me.*
PSALM 138:8, NASB

March

In the middle of the
muddle our holy Lord
is calmly at work.
—ELISABETH ELLIOT

God is our Helper. When the task He assigns is beyond our ability and we are totally helpless to fulfill it, He steps in and takes over. He does what we can't. His strength is perfect in our weakness.

ANNE GRAHAM LOTZ
God's Story

Whoever trusts
in the LORD, happy is he.
PROVERBS 16:20

Like peace, rest can be found only in one place, from one source, and that is the Lord Jesus Christ.

Jesus gives us the ultimate rest, the confidence we need, to escape the frustration and chaos of the world around us. Rest in Him and don't worry about what lies ahead. Jesus Christ has already taken care of tomorrow.

BILLY GRAHAM
Unto the Hills

ॐ

*Come to Me, all you who labor
. . . and I will give you rest.*
MATTHEW 11:28

God is magnanimous in mercy. He is generous in grace. He gives beyond anything you could ask or expect or hope for.

Even now He invites you into His presence for worship and praise and fellowship.

PETER WALLACE
What the Psalmist Is Saying

᠅

Because of your great mercy,
I come to your house, LORD, and I am filled
with wonder as I bow
down to worship at your holy temple.

PSALM 5:7, CEV

I n the Old Testament, the people who carried the Ark of the Covenant stopped every six steps to worship. We, too, need to remind ourselves not to go very far without stopping to worship. For spiritual well-being, we have to be six-step persons and continually invite the presence of the Lord to rule in our situations. We have to be free to praise Him no matter what our circumstances.

STORMIE OMARTIAN
Praying God's Will for Your Life

*Whoever offers praise
glorifies Me.*
PSALM 50:23

Perhaps you are passing through a wilderness right now. It may be the wilderness of a broken marriage, or a financial reversal, or a major disappointment, or a threatening illness.

But God is with you in the wilderness, and He goes before you to encourage and guide you. He brought the children of Israel through the wilderness—and He will bring you through it as well, as you look in faith to Him.

BILLY GRAHAM
Unto the Hills

*He is the living God,
and steadfast forever.*
DANIEL 6:26

God has gifted you with talents. He has done the same to your neighbor. If you concern yourself with your neighbor's talents, you will neglect yours. But if you concern yourself with yours, you could inspire both.

Max Lucado
He Still Moves Stones

ॐ

How precious also are Your thoughts to me,
O God! How great is the sum of them!
Psalm 139:17

79

March 7

Is "more" actually necessary? Is "upgrade" synonymous with godliness? . . . Where is that written? Yet we swallow the world's definition of "success" without hesitation.

Jesus did not swallow it. In fact, He tended to become invisible just when the crowds were about to name something after Him. He chose a cross over credentials, the marketplace over mansions, the people over their publicity.

ALICIA BRITT CHOLE
Pure Joy

❧

Your faith and hope are in God.
1 PETER 1:20–21, NIV

God's hand on your life may be just beginning to make its mark. That steep hill you've been climbing for such a long time may be the ramp to a destiny beyond your dreams. I do not believe there is any such thing as an accidental or ill-timed birth. You may have arrived in a home that was financially strapped. You may have known brokenness, hurt, and insecurity since your earliest days—but please hear me on this: *You were not an accident.*

CHARLES SWINDOLL
Moses: A Man of Selfless Dedication

ॐ

God is the strength of my heart.
PSALM 73:26

As God works with each human life, His attitude is that of the artist who is creating a masterpiece—not just for time—but for eternity. No positive value ever built into any human personality is wasted. Therefore, God can afford to take infinite, painstaking trouble with each of us. He can be just as patient in molding us according to His perfect pattern, as we force Him to be.

CATHERINE MARSHALL
Moments that Matter

❧

Commit your way to the LORD . . .
and He shall bring it to pass.
PSALM 37:5

Our spiritual journeys are lived moment by moment, not day by day or even week by week. God doles out our existence to us one breath at a time. To trust in our own means of survival and security instead of in God Himself is to miss out on God's serendipitous moments and events He has planned for us.

LESLIE WILLIAMS
Night Wrestling

❦

The LORD is my strength and my shield;
my heart trusted in Him, and I am helped.

PSALM 28:7

I wonder, how many burdens is Jesus carrying for us that we know nothing about? We're aware of some. He carries our sin. He carries our shame. He carries our eternal debt. But are there others? Has He lifted fears before we felt them? . . . Those times when we have been surprised by our own sense of peace? Could it be that Jesus has lifted our anxiety onto His shoulders and placed a yoke of kindness on ours?

MAX LUCADO
A Love Worth Giving

⌇

Take My yoke upon you . . . ,
and you will find rest for your souls.
MATTHEW 11:29

S pending time with God as I "walk" with Him meets needs that are in the deepest part of me. . . . And in some way I don't understand, I believe walking with me satisfies His heart. It brings Him pleasure to be loved and enjoyed and known just for Who He is. He is enthralled with the beauty of your character and mine as increasingly it reflects His own, and He rejoices over you and me.

ANNE GRAHAM LOTZ
God's Story

꙳

Because You have been my help, therefore in the shadow of Your wings I will rejoice.

PSALM 63:7

The Christian life must balance *receiving* and *giving*. The mind grows by taking in, but the heart grows by giving out; and the two activities must be balanced. Jesus urged, "Freely you have received, freely give." We can't give to others what we don't have; and what we have, we can get only from God.

WARREN W. WIERSBE
The 20 Essential Qualities

ॐ

*Freely you have
received, freely give.*
MATTHEW 10:8

March 14

We all have trouble seeing as God does because He looks through binoculars and we look through pinholes. He stands right next to us and says, "I see, I see, I know, I know."

We weren't created to "have our way" and "live our way." We were created to worship God and trust Him with His way.

KATHY TROCCOLI
Hope for a Woman's Heart

❧

Let all those who seek
You rejoice and be glad in You.
PSALM 70:4

March 15

All of our iniquities are carried away into the depths of the sea of God's forgiveness—not only to be buried from view but also forgotten forever. Only God our Father could be so gracious. Only He could be so magnanimous. Only He could be so utterly astonishing.

W. PHILLIP KELLER
Sea Edge

ॐ

He made Him who knew no sin
to be sin for us, that we might
become the righteousness of God in Him.

2 CORINTHIANS 5:21

We are conned—by advertising, by our needs, by our desire to play God in our own lives—into believing that planning is safety, that knowing the future is security. God has a plan for our lives, and He reveals it to us in His time, and only when He thinks we should know. To seek security in the future through any other means is idolatry.

LESLIE WILLIAMS
Night Wrestling

ॐ

God made everything
with a place and purpose.
PROVERBS 16:4, THE MESSAGE

Does bumping into certain people leave you brittle, breakable, and fruitless? If so, your love may be grounded in the wrong soil. It may be rooted in their love (which is fickle) or in your resolve to love (which is frail). John urges us to "rely on the love *God* has for us" (1 John 4:16, NIV). He alone is the power source.

MAX LUCADO
A Love Worth Giving

ॐ

*May your roots go down deep
into the soil of God's marvelous love.*

EPHESIANS 3:17, NLT

Living a grateful life is the art of paying attention to the details, of taking nothing for granted, and returning thanks for the smallest, the most hidden of God's blessings. Our blessings may be small or entirely hidden from view, but in them we find the door to God's kingdom.

HARRIET CROSBY
A Place Called Home

Let the peace of God rule
in your hearts, ...and be thankful.

COLOSSIANS 3:15

March 19

When God looks into the eyes of a woman, He sees all the beauty He created there. He sees every potential and every gift. He sees what can be and redeems what has been. He loves the curly hair that you wish were straight. He is taken with your smile and the shape of your nose. . . . He is the One who loves the inside *and* the outside of you. You were all His idea.

ANGELA THOMAS
Do You Think I'm Beautiful?

᠅

The LORD your God, . . . He will rejoice over you with gladness.

ZEPHANIAH 3:17

92

The Bible is God's love letter to you. When you receive letters from someone you love, you don't just read them once and never look at them again. You pore over them time after time, drinking in the very essence of that person, looking between the lines for any and every possible message. God's love letters to you are full of messages. They say, "This is how much I love you."

STORMIE OMARTIAN
Praying God's Will for Your Life

ॐ

So then faith comes by hearing,
and hearing by the word of God.
ROMANS 10:17

The sole light in Heaven will be the light that comes directly from God through Jesus Christ, and that light will be reflected in the life of each one of His children! The entire city will be saturated with the glory and light of life, truth, righteousness, goodness, love, and peace.

ANNE GRAHAM LOTZ
Heaven: My Father's House

❧

They need no lamp nor light of the sun,
for the Lord God gives them light.

REVELATION 22:5

Hope is bred in the bone. Our spirits were made for hope the way our hearts were made to love and our brains were made to think and our hands were made to make things. Our hearts are drawn to hope as an eagle is drawn to the sky.

LEWIS SMEDES
Keeping Hope Alive

*Happy is he who has the God
of Jacob for his help,
whose hope is in the LORD his God.*

PSALM 146:5

95

March 23

___

I f I satisfy my thirst for joy and passion by
the presence and the promises of Christ,
then the power of sin in my life is broken.
Dr. John Piper puts it this way, with a smile:
"We do not yield to the offer of sandwich
meat when we can smell the steak sizzling
on the grill."

And what whets our appetite for
maximum joy in the Lord? You guessed it—
God's Word.

JONI EARECKSON TADA
Holiness in Hidden Places

⌘

*I long for Your salvation,
O LORD, and Your law is my delight.*
PSALM 119:174

Recently I read someone's comment that "happiness is a talent." Even if you think you don't have a talent for happiness, *act* as if you do. You'll find that joy is like a vaccine that immunizes you against all sorts of maladies. Joy opens our hearts to see God's power at work in ourselves and in our world.

BARBARA JOHNSON
Leaking Laffs

❧

*Blessed are the people
who know the joyful sound!*
PSALM 89:15

97

Most of us are prone to think of God's will only as His plan for getting something done. That's why we pray, "Your will be done on earth as it is in heaven" (Matt. 6:10). Getting things done may be the *immediate* purpose of His will, but the *ultimate* purpose is His glory; and the glory of God is the highest purpose that can occupy the human heart and life.

WARREN W. WIERSBE
The 20 Essential Qualities

ॐ

You are our Father; . . .
we are the work of Your hand.

ISAIAH 64:8

March 26

What if everybody in the whole world decided to start looking at life through the lens of possibility? There would be no boring people. There would be no average days. . . . There would be no reason for prolonged discouragement—nothing to hold us back from conquering the enemies that steal our joy or disturb our souls. Everything would be possible because our focus would be on the Lord Jesus, who makes all things possible.

LUCI SWINDOLL
I Married Adventure

There has not failed
one word of all His good promise.
1 KINGS 8:56

God's passion always has been and always will be Jesus. Jesus is the entire heart of all God's stories.

Jesus is the heart of God's story in history. He is the heart of God's story in redemption, God's story in our present, God's story in our future. . . . He is not an addendum, an interesting footnote to God's work in the world. He is the center of all life and endeavor.

FAWN PARISH
It's All About You, Jesus

Because of His great love . . .
He . . . made us alive
together with Christ.
EPHESIANS 2:4–5

The weight of the cares that are laid on us is meticulously measured by the One who "knows our frame" and "knows full well that we are dust" (Ps. 103:14, NEB). Not a hair's weight more than we can sustain will be added to the load, but a load there must be for each of us, for we are in training.

We are promised something intriguing and mysterious when this is all over—"an eternal weight of glory, out of all proportion to our pain" (2 Cor. 4:17, NEB).

ELISABETH ELLIOT
The Music of His Promises

❧

*You have in heaven a better
and an enduring substance.*

HEBREWS 10:34, NEB

March 29

All gardens are living reminders of hope. When we plant a garden, we make real our hope that life will flourish and thrive. It is no accident that God created us in a garden. Eden was His promise that life would begin and continue in the midst of a world made of seas and dry land. In the garden God nurtured and loved His creatures.

When we plant a garden we imitate God.

HARRIET CROSBY
A Well-Watered Garden

Hope in the LORD; for with the LORD
there is mercy, and
with Him is abundant redemption.

PSALM 130:7

God works in your life as He does the earth. He waters you with the Spirit of joy. He enriches you with every spiritual nourishment you need. His river washes over you, cleansing you. He provides the grain of life, the necessities of sustenance. He waters your spirit abundantly, showering you with peace, blessing your growth.

PETER WALLACE
What the Psalmist Is Saying

❧

You take care of the earth
and send rain to help the soil grow
all kinds of crops.
PSALM 65:9–10, CEV

103

The home you've always wanted, the home you continue to long for with all your heart, is the home God is preparing for you! As John gazed at a vision of the glory of Jesus Christ . . . , he stood in awed wonder of "a new heaven and a new earth" (Rev. 21:1, NIV). What he saw was confirmed by the words of One Who was seated on the throne: "I am making everything new!" Imagine it: One day, in the dream home of My Father's House, *everything* will be brand-new!

ANNE GRAHAM LOTZ
Heaven: My Father's House

૱

"I am making everything new!"
REVELATION 21:5, NIV

God is infinitely good, and therefore infinitely loving.

—FULTON J. SHEEN

What does your song in the night sound like? It could be a mournful dirge. Or a staccato outburst. Or a stirring song of praise.

But those nights when you can't sleep, when your mind speeds out of control, rummaging through the problems and trials of your life, you can slow things down with a song or a meditation. Direct your mind toward God.

PETER WALLACE
What the Psalmist Is Saying

∽

*I call to remembrance my song
in the night; I meditate within my heart.*

PSALM 77:6

Who I am is God's gift to me, yes. However, what I make of myself is also God's gift to me. God has given me the education, the opportunities, the encouragement, the discipline to become who I am. Everything is a gift. I must make the decision to follow Jesus Christ, but after that, my service to God is really one more gift He gives me.

W. PHILLIP KELLER
Sea Edge

❧

Let Your hand become my help,
for I have chosen Your precepts.
PSALM 119:173

Worship is the act of magnifying God. Enlarging our vision of Him. Stepping into the cockpit to see where He sits and observe how He works. Of course, His size doesn't change, but our perception of Him does. As we draw nearer, He seems larger. Isn't that what we need? A *big* view of God?

MAX LUCADO
Just Like Jesus

Oh, magnify the LORD with me,
and let us exalt His name together.

PSALM 34:3

Happiness is a byproduct of something greater, not an end in itself. Happiness cannot be pursued and caught, anymore than one can pursue a sunny day, put it in a bottle, and then bring it out on a rainy day to enjoy again.

True happiness comes from a different pursuit—the pursuit of God.

BILLY GRAHAM
Unto the Hills

You will seek Me and find Me,
when you search for Me with all your heart.

JEREMIAH 29:13

April 5

You know what? God personally cares about the things that worry us. He cares more about them than we care about them: those things that hang in our minds as nagging, aching, worrisome thoughts. . . . He cares. You are His personal concern.

CHARLES SWINDOLL
Perfect Trust

~

Casting all your care
upon Him, for He cares for you.
1 PETER 5:7

God's love for you is so individual, Jesus told us He even has the hairs of your head numbered. Well, since that's true, surely He knows every little thing about each one of us and wants us to ask for His help with every little thing. But He does insist that we ask. Having had the courage and audacity to give us free will, God respects that always and forever. He will not crash the door of our hearts.

CATHERINE MARSHALL
Moments that Matter

༈

*The very hairs of
your head are all numbered.*
MATTHEW 10:30

Faith, in one sense, is simply a *readiness* for God. A kind of emptiness waiting to be filled, the way an empty cup held out by a beggar is ready to be filled. Or the way eaglets, with beaks open wider than the width of their bodies, wait for the mother eagle to fly back to the nest with food in her mouth. What God puts in the mouths of our faith is Himself.

LEWIS SMEDES
Keeping Hope Alive

᠅

I have trusted in Your mercy;
my heart shall rejoice in Your salvation.
PSALM 13:5

God loves you simply because He has chosen to do so.

He loves you when you don't feel lovely.

He loves you when no one else loves you.

Others may abandon you, divorce you, and ignore you, but God will love you. Always. No matter what.

MAX LUCADO
A Love Worth Giving

My soul shall be joyful
in the LORD; it shall rejoice in His salvation.

PSALM 35:9

113

Worry is a habit, and just like any other habit cannot be gotten rid of by simply wishing it would go away. In *The Imitation of Christ*, Thomas á Kempis said, "Habit is overcome by habit." The old habit of worry must be replaced by the new habit of trust.

LESLIE WILLIAMS
Night Wrestling

روح

To You, O LORD, I lift up my soul.
O my God, I trust in You.

PSALM 25:1

When pain and problems press us up against a holy God, guess what goes first? You've got it. The selfishness that pain unmasks. The pride and pettiness that problems reveal.

The beauty of being stripped down to the basics is that God can then fill us up with Himself.

JONI EARECKSON TADA
Holiness in Hidden Places

༄

You died, and your life
is hidden with Christ in God.
COLOSSIANS 3:3

If you keep in mind that discerning the will of God means developing a personal relationship with the Lord—not receiving a series of memos from heaven—then you will better understand how this demanding but delightful process works. The better we get to know the Lord, the better we understand His ways and His character and, therefore, the better we know how to please Him.

WARREN W. WIERSBE
The 20 Essential Qualities

ઝ

Teach me Your way,
O LORD; I will walk in Your truth.
PSALM 86:11

When we need a miracle, we usually get lost in the morass of the situation we're in or the overwhelming odds before us. But imagine being lost, completely lost, in the wonder of God. What a great place to be! When this happens, our prayers become focused on God, not on our problem.

JOHN HULL AND TIM ELMORE
Pivotal Praying

⁓

I have heard your prayer,
I have seen your tears.

ISAIAH 38:5

In the Christian life, freedom isn't the
privilege of doing whatever we please,
because living to please only ourselves would
be the worst bondage possible. Rather,
freedom means life controlled by truth and
motivated by love. We not only speak "the
truth in love," but we seek to live the truth
in love by the power of the Spirit of God.

WARREN W. WIERSBE
The 20 Essential Qualities

࿔

We should . . . [speak] the truth in love.

EPHESIANS 4:14–15

B ased on our knowing God and His
character, we can say, with confidence:
God has a plan for my future that is good
and not evil.
God will never leave me or forsake me.
God loves me with an undying love.
God is faithful to forgive my sins.
God will keep His promises.

KATHY TROCCOLI
Hope for a Woman's Heart

う

If we are faithless, He remains faithful;
He cannot deny Himself.
2 TIMOTHY 2:13

I f God is the Destination of our spiritual journey, then we are freed from the fear of making bad choices. The present moment is all that matters. The future snuggles right into the present, and gives us peace.

LESLIE WILLIAMS
Night Wrestling

∽

You are my lamp, O LORD;
the LORD shall enlighten my darkness.
2 SAMUEL 22:29

120

The Shepherd speaks to us personally—by name. . . .

He knows our thoughts before they're on our minds, our words before they're formed on our tongues, our emotions before they're felt in our hearts, and our actions before there is any movement. When He speaks, it's in the language of our own personal lives, through a verse or passage of Scripture that just seems to leap up off the page with our name on it.

ANNE GRAHAM LOTZ
My Heart's Cry

᳀

I am the good shepherd; and I know
My sheep, and am known by My own.

JOHN 10:14

During the cold and rainy times of your life, God has shown Himself to be a safe, warm, dry shelter. So you can trust Him now for whatever you need.

In His strong tower, you are removed from the enemy's battle below. You are protected from attack, safe from harm.

PETER WALLACE
What the Psalmist Is Saying

❧

You are a strong tower,
where I am safe from my enemies.

PSALM 61:3, CEV

April 18

I t takes time to draw aside from society. It takes time to enter deliberately into the presence of God. It takes time to commune with Christ as friend.

It demands a deliberate act of faith that in such a spot I shall meet my God. In His presence my soul finds strength, my days find deep delight.

W. PHILLIP KELLER
Sea Edge

๛

He raises the poor out of the dust,
and lifts the needy out of the ash heap.

PSALM 113:7

123

True friendships are characterized by grace, truth, forgiveness, unselfishness, and love in gigantic and mutual proportion. Although they require hard work and consistency from each party, we enjoy the best of the best in life because when friends come alongside, more light is added to our path. Two are better than one! We lay down our lives for our friends, they lay down their lives for us, and in the end we all find true life.

LUCI SWINDOLL
I Married Adventure

ॐ

Greater love has no one than this,
than to lay down one's life for his friends.
JOHN 15:13

Waiting on God is an act of faith—the greatest thing ever required of us humans. Not faith in the outcome we are dictating to God, but faith in His character, faith in Himself. It is resting in the perfect confidence that He will guide in the right way, at the right time. He will supply our need. He will fulfill His word. He will give us the very best if we trust Him.

ELISABETH ELLIOT
The Path of Loneliness

∾

If you have faith as a mustard seed, . . .
nothing will be impossible for you.
MATTHEW 17:20

It's difficult for me to understand how God can look at me, with all my failures and sins, hold me close to His heart, and love me with exuberant joy—but He does. He can joyfully delight in His people because we're in His Son; and when the Father looks at His Son, He says, "This is My beloved Son, in whom I am well pleased" (Matt. 3:17). Paul calls this "accepted in the Beloved."

WARREN W. WIERSBE
The 20 Essential Qualities

෨

He made us accepted in the Beloved.

EPHESIANS 1:6

When placed in the light of our awesome God, our lives find new perspective:

Anxiety is replaced by hope when we see that nothing could ever be bigger than God.

Fear looses its strength when we recognize that God's power and love are a million times greater than our weakness and failure.

ALICIA BRITT CHOLE
Pure Joy

Perfect love casts out fear.

1 JOHN 4:18

127

April 23

The eagle is the only bird that can lock its wings and wait for the right wind. It waits for the updraft and never has to flap its wings—just soar. So as we wait on God, He will help us use the adversities and strong winds of life to our benefit!

BILLY GRAHAM
Unto the Hills

ॐ

Those who wait upon GOD get fresh strength.
They spread their wings and soar like eagles.
ISAIAH 40:31, *THE MESSAGE*

God has been intimately acquainted with each human soul since the beginning of time. He looks upon the world and sees billions of individuals, one at a time. Each heart, each mind, each soul— He knows them personally. Intimately. Because He fashioned each one individually.

PETER WALLACE
What the Psalmist Is Saying

He fashions their hearts individually;
He considers all their works.

PSALM 33:15

On the human level, one of love's most obvious characteristics is unselfishness. The mother does not think of herself, but of the welfare of those she loves.

Since God is all love, . . . can His love be of a different caliber? The truth is that God is not only unselfish; He is *selfless*. His every thought, purpose, and plan since the beginning of time, has been for His children's welfare and happiness.

CATHERINE MARSHALL
Moments that Matter

༉

God is love.
1 JOHN 4:16

You will never be completely happy on earth simply because you were not made for earth. Oh, you will have your moments of joy. You will catch glimpses of light. You will know moments or even days of peace. But they simply do not compare with the happiness that lies ahead.

MAX LUCADO
When God Whispers Your Name

న

My kingdom does not belong to this world.
JOHN 18:36, NCV

Jesus wants us to follow His goals before we choose our roles. He calls us to His cause before our career. Instead of pursuing the elusive value of freedom, He offers us the reality of a fruit-bearing friendship. Instead of seeking a fading self-fulfillment, Jesus offers us the genuine experience of "followship."

STEVE HAWTHORNE
Perspectives

Jesus said, "Come follow me."
MATTHEW 4:19, NCV

April 28

There will always be conditions in our lives that are not to our liking. "If only I had . . . if only this . . . if only he would . . ." If our hearts are set on visible and temporal things we shall be irremediably miserable. It is a fractured world. But if we look up beyond the causes of our discontent to the invisible and the eternal, we shall learn to be contented "with such things as we have" (Heb. 13:5, NEB).

ELISABETH ELLIOT
The Music of His Promises

ॐ

Be relaxed with what you have.
HEBREWS 13:5, *THE MESSAGE*

God's Word is not *Basic Instructions Before Leaving Earth*. It is the revelation of a person in His fascinating multi-layered personality. The Word of God is not a code of conduct; it is not a list of rules; it certainly is not a compilation of unconnected stories. It is a treasure map, and Jesus is the treasure.

FAWN PARISH
It's All About You, Jesus

*His divine power has given to us
all things that pertain to life and godliness.*

2 PETER 1:3

The Bible tells us not to hide our lights under a bushel, to show forth our good works so that we might glorify our Father in heaven. The trick is to do our good works with gratitude, not pride; otherwise, we worship the work and our part in it instead of God.

LESLIE WILLIAMS
Seduction of the Lesser Gods

❧

*Let your light so shine before men,
that they may see your good
works and glorify your Father in heaven.*
MATTHEW 5:16

135

May

A little love
can change a life.
—MAX LUCADO

May 1

When I asked my pastor how he defined a confident woman, he said, "She knows where she's going. She's got her orders straight." Then he gave me this wonderful definition of *submission:* in Latin it means "one who is sent under orders." I believe that when we listen to the gentle Shepherd, He also guides us in our personal goals. God wants only the best for us. He likes to treat each one of us as if we were an only child.

INGRID TROBISCH
The Confident Woman

꒰

Trust . . . in the living God,
who gives us richly all things to enjoy.
1 TIMOTHY 6:17

I n all honesty, we know how little genuine love we bring to God even in moments of what is supposed to be worship, how feebly and selectively we love our neighbor. The love God demands can only be the gift of God. Yet He cannot give us that gift so long as bitterness and resentment have slammed shut the door of the heart.

Forgiveness is the precondition to love.

CATHERINE MARSHALL
Moments that Matter

*You shall love the LORD your God
with all your heart. . . .
You shall love your neighbor as yourself.*
MARK 12:30–31

S unset is an hour for quiet reflection.
There can be no replay of the day,
except in fleeting memory. There can be no
rewriting of the script etched upon these
hours. With the indelible ink of eternity
there has been inscribed upon the page of
this eternal sheet of time either something
of value, or only what is vain.

W. PHILLIP KELLER
Sea Edge

❧

The things which are seen are temporary,
but the things which are not seen are eternal.
2 CORINTHIANS 4:18

God is *for* you. Turn to the sidelines; that's God cheering your run. Look past the finish line; that's God applauding your steps. Listen for Him in the bleachers, shouting your name. Too tired to continue? He'll carry you. Too discouraged to fight? He's picking you up. God is for you.

MAX LUCADO
In the Grip of Grace

∾

Yet I will rejoice in the LORD,
I will joy in the God of my salvation.
HABAKKUK 3:18

God deserves preeminence in our lives.
He is the source of our strength
and wholeness.

He is the beginning and the end of all
that we are and ever will be.

He has redeemed us and nurtured us.
And He loves us more than an earthly
parent ever could.

PETER WALLACE
What the Psalmist Is Saying

ɔ

You are my God. I worship you.

PSALM 63:1, CEV

How could any of us who have embarked on the pilgrimage that is Christianity do without the Holy Spirit? For we who long for something more, for strength and hope and wisdom beyond ourselves, discover to our joy that as the Comforter reveals Christ to us, in Him we have our heart's desire.

CATHERINE MARSHALL
Moments that Matter

✿

The Spirit of truth . . .
dwells with you and will be in you.
JOHN 14:17

143

It is the goodness and kindness of God that lead us to repentance. This goes against everything ingrained in us. We want to be punished when we fail. We want to pay, then we feel released from our guilt. But God extends His mercy to cover what should be our judgment. . . .

You have confessed, now you must go from the place of sin. . . . God says you are not condemned. You must walk in that truth.

LISA BEVERE
Be Angry but Don't Blow It!

༄

God's kindness leads you toward repentance.

ROMANS 2:4, NIV

You don't have to be like the world to have an impact on the world. You don't have to be like the crowd to change the crowd. You don't have to lower yourself down to their level to lift them up to your level. Holiness doesn't seek to be odd. Holiness seeks to be like God.

MAX LUCADO
A Gentle Thunder

God is doing what is best for us,
training us to live God's holy best.
ROMANS 12:10, *THE MESSAGE*

May 9

A cry for forgiveness is a cry for mercy—
that in spite of whatever sins we have
committed, we beg to rest in God's undying
love for us. Having received mercy and
pardon for our sins, we extend forgiveness
to those who have wronged us.

HARRIET CROSBY
A Place Called Home

✍

*If we confess our sins, He is faithful
and just to forgive us our sins
and to cleanse us from all unrighteousness.*

1 JOHN 1:9

God has included the hardships of my life (which I confess have been *few*) in His original plan. Nothing takes Him by surprise. But nothing is for nothing, either. His plan is to make me holy, and hardship is indispensable for that as long as we live in this hard old world. All I have to do is accept it.

ELISABETH ELLIOT
The Path of Loneliness

☙

You are my hope, O LORD GOD;
You are my trust from my youth.

PSALM 71:5

P raise is the switch that turns on the light of joy in our lives even when it is "dark" outside. And the resulting "light" causes others to see the glory of God in our lives. As my life gets more complicated and my problems and pressures seem to have become permanent fixtures, I want to turn on the "light."

ANNE GRAHAM LOTZ
My Heart's Cry

⁓

Rejoice in the Lord always.
I will say it again: Rejoice!
PHILIPPIANS 4:4, NIV

"Let us make man in our image," God said. The image we bear is not composed of facial or external features. It can rarely be said that we have our Father's eyes. It is not as if we walk, run, or hold our head similar to the way God does. Oh no! It is that our being is made like Him. We were made a trinity: body, soul, and spirit. We were made for indivisible relationship with Him and with each other. We were made to be a part of Him and of each other.

FAWN PARISH
It's All About You, Jesus

ॐ

He will teach us His ways,
and we shall walk in His paths.

ISAIAH 2:3

149

L ife is full of serendipitous and surprising detours—not all of them easily accepted at the moment. . . . Usually, we're minding our own business and, quite suddenly, we encounter the unexpected. These things happen in our lives every day, and we have the choice to either embrace our experience with a sense of trust or spend our energies fighting the inevitable. We can respond to challenges and opportunities with "Why me?" or . . . with "Why not?"

LUCI SWINDOLL
I Married Adventure

৵

*In Your hand it is to make great
and to give strength to all.*
1 CHRONICLES 29:12

May 14

Regardless of your present circumstances or crisis, pressures or pain, suffering or sorrow, failures or frustrations, danger or disease, . . . your situation is temporary compared to eternity. And eternity is going to be spent with Jesus in His Father's house that has been lovingly prepared just for you!

ANNE GRAHAM LOTZ
My Heart's Cry

꙼

He rules by His power forever; . . .
Oh, bless our God, you peoples!
PSALM 66:7–8

151

To live *circumspectly* means to live with the realization that the whole of our lives is connected. We are charged to live our lives, weighing our decisions and actions from every angle and point of view. We need to take a walk around our decisions, visit every room, and be certain we like the way it looks and feels from every angle before we commit ourselves to it long term.

LISA BEVERE
Kissed the Girls

ॐ

See then that you walk circumspectly,
not as fools but as wise.
EPHESIANS 5:15

May 16

True humility is not thinking lowly of yourself but thinking accurately of yourself. The humble heart does not say, "I can't do anything." But rather, "I can't do everything. I know my part and am happy to do it."

MAX LUCADO
A Love Worth Giving

Do nothing out of selfish ambition
or vain conceit, but in humility
consider others better than yourselves.
PHILIPPIANS 2:3, NIV

153

I have always thought it ironic that Jesus spent His blood-sweating agony not on an ash heap like Job, or in the desert like the Israelites, but instead among blossoms and fresh scent of cedar and olive trees. After the Last Supper, He did not choose to impart more wisdom to His disciples; He did not choose to be in intimate contact with those He loved the most. He chose to be alone with God in a garden.

LESLIE WILLIAMS
Night Wrestling

༔

*Blessed be God, Who has not
turned away my prayer,
nor His mercy from me!*
PSALM 66:20

Daily, hourly, momentarily Christ comes to us surrounding us with His spirit. He brings to us in immeasurable abundance the resources needed for our eternal living. Yet there remains my responsibility to open myself to Him; to allow His Word ready entry to my mind, emotions and will; to permit His Spirit to invade my spirit.

W. Phillip Keller
Sea Edge

ॐ

He has made His wonderful
works to be remembered.

Psalm 111:4

May 19

Even in the most raging waters of life, our Lord's hand will guide us and will hold us fast. Even in our darkest moments, the Lord is illuminating and clear. We often wonder, "Do You know what You're doing?" Yes, He does. We can be sure of it. God speaks to us often and says, "Let Me worry about that."

KATHY TROCCOLI
Hope for a Woman's Heart

~

Blessed are all who put their trust in Him.

PSALM 2:12

S ome folks believe we can know God without being known by the people of God. But Jesus did not offer Christianity for independent study. He was committed to the gathered people of God. . . . Jesus was committed to the gathered people of God because God is committed to us, and He has committed us to one another. Christianity is lived in the plural, not the singular.

ALICIA BRITT CHOLE
Pure Joy

⌘

The way of the LORD
is strength for the upright.
PROVERBS 10:29

May 21

Imagine considering every moment as a potential time of communion with God. By the time your life is over, you will have spent six months at stoplights, eight months opening junk mail, a year and a half looking for lost stuff . . . , and a whopping five years standing in various lines.

Why don't you give these moments to God?

MAX LUCADO
Just Like Jesus

∽

And He said, "My presence will
go with you and I will give you rest."
EXODUS 33:14

Godly people possess an attitude of willing submission to God's will and ways. Whatever He says goes. And whatever it takes to carry it out is the very thing the godly desire to do.

CHARLES SWINDOLL
The Finishing Touch

*Take my yoke upon you
and learn from Me.*

MATTHEW 11:29

God's gift of love and forgiveness means that we don't have to scrounge for scraps of attention or affection; that we can be mulish and stubborn, and God loves us anyway; that we don't have to sip the bitter tea of revenge until we make ourselves sick; that our unfulfilled desires won't kill us in the end; that we can give our second-rate plans to God, and He will sanctify our lives.

LESLIE WILLIAMS
Seduction of the Lesser Gods

ॐ

You have forgiven the iniquity
of Your people; You have covered all their sin.

PSALM 85:2

Life is too short for us to be carrying grudges. Have you planned to write that letter or make that phone call, but somehow it just hasn't gotten done? Then do it! It wouldn't hurt if every single day we expressed our sincere appreciation to somebody in our circle who means something to us.

WARREN W. WIERSBE
The 20 Essential Qualities

〜

Our Father in heaven . . . keep us forgiven with you and forgiving others.
MATTHEW 6:10–12, THE MESSAGE

May 25

Self-control is included in the list of fruits of the Spirit. *Self*-control. The Holy Spirit does not do all the controlling for us. He requires us to act. He helps us, but He expects us to cooperate. If we begin each day by an acknowledgment of our dependence upon Him, and our intention to obey Him, He will certainly help us.

ELISABETH ELLIOT
The Path of Loneliness

~

The fruit of the Spirit is . . . self-control.
GALATIANS 5:22–23

You and I can be where Jesus is—now, and for all eternity—because He lives within us and has promised that He will never leave us nor forsake us! When you and I follow Jesus, He promises that we will be where He is. And there is not one place in the entire universe, visible or invisible, where He is not! What a blessing!

ANNE GRAHAM LOTZ
My Heart's Cry

I will never leave you nor forsake you.

HEBREWS 13:5

163

Even when we don't know how to pray, the Holy Spirit knows our needs, and He brings the deepest cries of our hearts before the throne of God. In ways we will never understand this side of eternity, God the Holy Spirit pleads for us before God the Father.

Turn to God in every situation—even when you don't feel like it. The Spirit is interceding for you, in accordance with God's will.

BILLY GRAHAM
Unto the Hills

᠅

The Spirit intercedes
for the saints in accordance with God's will.
ROMANS 8:27, NIV

When we surrender to God the cumbersome sack of discontent, we don't just give up something; we gain something. God replaces it with a lightweight, tailor-made, sorrow-resistant attaché of gratitude.

What will you gain with contentment? You may gain your marriage. You may gain precious hours with your children. You may gain joy.

MAX LUCADO
Traveling Light

ॐ

Godliness with contentment is great gain.

1 TIM. 6:6, NIV

May 29

God is kind. He overflows with love toward you, taking your needs and hurts to heart, working all things together for good on your behalf. He is merciful, full of mercy and grace toward you, and not because of anything you have done to earn His acceptance. He is slow to anger. His patience is limitless. His love is limitless.

PETER WALLACE
What the Psalmist Is Saying

༃

But you, the LORD God, are kind and merciful. . . .
Your love can always be trusted.

PSALM 86:15, CEV

May 30

I n the wilderness of loneliness we are
  terribly vulnerable. What we want is
OUT, and sometimes there appear some easy
ways to get there. Will we take Satan up on
his offers, satisfy our desires in ways never
designed by God, seek security outside of
His holy will? If we do, we may find a
measure of happiness, but not the lasting joy
our heavenly Father wants us to have.

ELISABETH ELLIOT
The Path of Loneliness

~

God is our refuge and strength,
a very present help in trouble.
PSALM 46:1

To abide in Christ means to remain connected to Him so completely that the "sap" of His Spirit flows through every part of your being, including your mind, will, and emotions as well as your words and deeds. The "fruit" that you then bear is actually produced by His Spirit in you through no conscious effort of your own. If you and I want to be fruitful, we do not concentrate on fruit-bearing; we concentrate on our personal relationship with Jesus Christ.

ANNE GRAHAM LOTZ
My Heart's Cry

❧

Abide in me, and I in you.
As the branch cannot bear fruit of itself.

JOHN 15:4

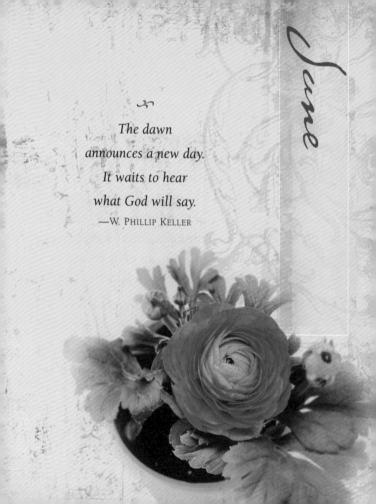

*The dawn
announces a new day.
It waits to hear
what God will say.*
—W. PHILLIP KELLER

When we have Jesus, we indeed have everything. All that God demands of us is met in Jesus. He is the supremely all-sufficient One, the first and last, the living One. Our greatest need, and God's greatest gift to us, is to awaken us to the sufficiency, supremacy, and destiny of the Lord Jesus Christ. We are called to an undistracted and lifelong preoccupation with Him.

FAWN PARISH
It's All About You, Jesus

⌘

No good thing will He
withhold from those who walk uprightly.

PSALM 84:11

This world is not out of control, spinning wildly through space. Nor are earth's inhabitants at the mercy of some blind, random fate. When God created the world and set the stars in space, He also established the course of this world and His plan for humanity.

CHARLES SWINDOLL
The Mystery of God's Will

๛

O LORD my God, You are very great; . . .
You who laid the foundations of the earth.
PSALM 104:1,5

Miracles happen right in front of us and we do not even notice. And these miracles are the really big ones. Not the lame walking or the blind seeing—those receive our attention—but the miracle of the lost being sought by the Great Shepherd. We miss the miracle of God knocking on the door of a human heart.

ALICIA BRITT CHOLE
Pure Joy

᠅

I have loved you with an everlasting love;
therefore with loving-kindness
I have drawn you.

JEREMIAH 31:3

From Genesis to Revelation, from earth's greatest tragedy to earth's greatest triumph, the dramatic story of humanity's lowest depths and God's highest heights can be couched in twenty-five beautiful words: "For God so loved the world that He gave His only begotten Son, that whoever believes in Him should not perish but have everlasting life" (John 3:16).

BILLY GRAHAM
Unto the Hills

❦

*In this the love of God was made manifest...,
that God sent his only Son into the world.*

1 JOHN 4:9–10, NRSV

You have a God who hears you, the power of love behind you, the Holy Spirit within you, and all of heaven ahead of you. If you have the Shepherd, you have grace for every sin, direction for every turn, a candle for every corner, and an anchor for every storm. You have everything you need.

MAX LUCADO
Traveling Light

ॐ

The LORD is my shepherd; I shall not want.
PSALM 23:1

When God acts, it is because He himself has taken the initiative and made the decision to do so.

God took the initiative to create the universe . . . to create the Earth . . . to create man . . . to create woman. . . . And God took the initiative to send His own Son to earth to be our Savior.

ANNE GRAHAM LOTZ
God's Story

෨

God so loved the world,
that he gave his one and only Son,
that whoever believes in him
shall not perish but have eternal life.

JOHN 3:16, NIV

Every day, we are literally overwhelmed by an abundance of goodness from the hand of God: relationships that bring joy and support, activities that provide an outlet for giving and growth, an eternal relationship with God. He not only loads us with benefits but also carries our burdens. At our invitation, He takes the weight of sadness and fear in our lives upon Himself.

PETER WALLACE
What the Psalmist Is Saying

ॐ

Blessed be the LORD,
Who daily loads us with benefits.

PSALM 68:19

Any time you struggle with negative emotions, such as anger, . . . fear, hurt, depression, or worthlessness, thank God that He is bigger than all that. Thank Him that His plans and purposes for you are good. Thank Him that in any weak area of your life, He will be strong. Thank Him that He came to restore you.

STORMIE OMARTIAN
Praying God's Will for Your Life

❧

Oh, give thanks to the LORD, for He is good!
For His mercy endures forever.

PSALM 136:1

June 9

In circumstances for which there is no final answer in the world, we have two choices: accept them as God's wise and loving choice for our blessing (this is called faith), or resent them as proof of His indifference, His carelessness, even His non-existence (this is unbelief).

ELISABETH ELLIOT
The Path of Loneliness

᷒

We have access by faith into
this grace in which we stand,
and rejoice in hope of the glory of God.

ROMANS 5:2

The great freedom Jesus gives us is to be ourselves, defined by His love and our inner qualities and gifts rather than by any kind of show we put on for the world. We are freed, like uncaged birds, because God loves us unconditionally—without degrees, promotions, elected offices, or a cool crowd surrounding us.

LESLIE WILLIAMS
Seduction of the Lesser Gods

*The love of God
has been poured out in our hearts.*

ROMANS 5:5

179

Trusting God means thinking and acting according to God's Word in spite of circumstances, feelings, or consequences. The object of our faith is God—not our feelings, not faith itself, but almighty God.

WARREN W. WIERSBE
The 20 Essential Qualities

We walk by faith, not by sight.

2 CORINTHIANS 5:7

In heaven we won't be encumbered by all the material goods that clutter our lives here on earth. Whatever their size, our heavenly homes will be places of love set in neighborhoods where the peace is never interrupted by police or ambulance sirens, storm warnings, or blaring security alarms. How wonderful it is to picture the happy life we'll know for all eternity. How comforting it is to know we'll share it with our friends and loved ones who are waiting for us there.

BARBARA JOHNSON
He's Gonna Toot

❧

Keep yourselves in the love of God,
looking for the mercy of
our Lord Jesus Christ unto eternal life.
JUDE 20

The bonds that unite families and friends are not forged for a little while, they are for eternity. They stretch across every boundary of space and time. They twine and intertwine from one generation to another, weave and interweave, priceless beyond measure. They are something to be cherished, to be fought for, to be kept intact at all cost.

CATHERINE MARSHALL
Moments that Matter

*This is My commandment, that
you love one another as I have loved you.*
JOHN 15:12

Does God love us because of our goodness? Because of our kindness? Because of our great faith? No, He loves us because of *His* goodness, kindness, and great faith. John says it like this: "This is love: not that we loved God, but that he loved us."

MAX LUCADO
A Love Worth Giving

*This is love: not that we loved God,
but that he loved us.*

1 JOHN 4:10, NIV

June 15

We keep changing the bandages instead of running to God and saying, "Heal me, Lord—whatever it takes." We hide and we keep on hiding. Like Adam and Eve, God speaks to us: "Why are you doing that? I see it all." He wants us to come to Him with abandon.

KATHY TROCCOLI
Hope for a Woman's Heart

Blessed are the pure in heart,
for they shall see God.

MATTHEW 5:8

Real love doesn't abandon. . . . Lovers might. Friends might. Children might. But God doesn't.

Whether we return the embrace or not, Jesus Christ stands with His arms open, day in and day out. Real love knows us completely and forgives us completely. Real love never turns away, ever.

LESLIE WILLIAMS
Seduction of the Lesser Gods

ॐ

I will look to the LORD; I will wait
for the God of my salvation;
my God will hear me.

MICAH 7:7

Surely we have misunderstood Christianity if we think God wants us to obey Him reluctantly and fearfully—resisting, bucking, hating every step of the way. Jesus came to show us a new way by which God promises to work in us "both to will and to do of His good pleasure."

This means that God will bring about such a change in us that His plans and desires for us will be our delight.

CATHERINE MARSHALL
Moments that Matter

࿐

*It is your Father's good pleasure
to give you the kingdom.*
LUKE 12:32

Love is a fruit. A fruit of whom? Of your hard work? Of your deep faith? Of your rigorous resolve? No. Love is a fruit of the Spirit of God. "The Spirit produces the fruit" (Gal. 5:22, NCV).

MAX LUCADO
A Love Worth Giving

∾

The fruit of the Spirit is love, joy, peace.

GALATIANS 5:22

187

Discouragement is a large cloud that, like all clouds, obscures the warmth and joy of the sun. . . .

There is only one way to dispel discouragement, and it is not in our own strength or ingenuity. It is to turn in faith to God, believing that He loves us and is in control of the future. The Bible says, "Wait on the LORD . . . and He shall strengthen your heart."

BILLY GRAHAM
Unto the Hills

ॐ

Wait on the LORD; be of good courage,
and He shall strengthen your heart.

PSALM 27:14

The mystery of God's identity as three Persons in One is hard to comprehend. One classic illustration is that of water, which retains its key . . . properties but can appear as liquid, steam, or ice. While God's Personhood and power do not change, He reveals Himself as Father, Son (living Word), and Spirit. Although no explanation is totally satisfying, we can worship the God Who, if small enough for us to understand, would not be big enough to . . . be worthy of our worship.

ANNE GRAHAM LOTZ
God's Story

༣

There are three that bear witness in heaven: the Father, the Word, and the Holy Spirit: and these three are one.

1 JOHN 5:7

When life comes undone, when pretending is not an option anymore, when everything has fallen apart and fallen away, amazingly, it all becomes very simple. When no one can do anything to help and there isn't a straw left to grasp or a mask left to hide behind, God gets to move center stage. He has our undivided attention. The questions that we've held out to everyone remain, but there is no one to answer except Him.

ANGELA THOMAS
Do You Think I'm Beautiful?

ॐ

Trust in the LORD with all your heart,
and lean not on your own understanding.

PROVERBS 3:5

To be content in whatever state we are is the wisdom to accept with gratitude the experience of *not* having what we wish for. Mark this well. We *cannot* be content with the way things are as long as things are not the way we wish them to be. But we *can* be content to live with our discontent until things get to be the way we hope they will be.

LEWIS SMEDES
Keeping Hope Alive

๛

*I have learned in whatever state I am,
to be content: I know how to be abased,
and I know how to abound.*
PHILIPPIANS 4:11–12

God Himself is not *in* a sunset or *in* an act of human compassion any more than an artist is in his painting or a musician is in his music. . . .God is separate from His creation. This means: When something is wrong, He can right it. When something is broken, He can mend it. When something is lost, He can find it. When something is hurt, He can heal it.

ANNE GRAHAM LOTZ
God's Story

ᘿ

All things were made through Him,
and without Him
nothing was made that was made.

JOHN 1:3

"Your life is now hidden with Christ in God." The Chinese language has a great symbol for this truth. The word for *righteousness* is a combination of two pictures. On the top is a lamb. Beneath the lamb is a person. The lamb covers the person. Isn't that the essence of righteousness? The Lamb of Christ over the child of God? Whenever the Father looks down on you . . . He sees His Son, the perfect Lamb of God, hiding you.

MAX LUCADO
A Love Worth Giving

~

Your life is now hidden
with Christ in God.

COLOSSIANS 3:3, NIV

Though fate may be fickle, God is not. God is constant, ready to hold our hands as we lurch, tiptoe, stride into uncertainty, and to hold us in His arms when disaster catches us off-guard, or to shield us when our expectations explode with good news. God is with us no matter what future we wake up in.

LESLIE WILLIAMS
Night Wrestling

જી

Has not the LORD gone out before you?
JUDGES 4:14

The ability to get a laugh out of everyday situations is a safety valve. It rids us of tensions and worries that could otherwise damage our health.

What is it that brings healing to the emotions, healing to the soul? A joyful heart!

CHARLES SWINDOLL
Living Above the Level of Mediocrity

A joyful heart is good medicine.

PROVERBS 17:22, NASB

I f you are in the midst of a storm that has suddenly taken a turn for the worse, look up! Your Savior sees you where you are and will come to you. He will give you peace through His Word in the midst of the storm. Open your Bible and read what He has to say. And if you pray and invite Him into the "boat" of your life . . . He will come in and still the storm.

ANNE GRAHAM LOTZ
God's Story

❧

The righteous shall be
glad in the LORD, and trust in Him.
PSALM 64:10

I would like to suggest that "being one" is not about the absence of difference but about the presence of commitment. We are committed to one another as an overflow of our common commitment to Jesus. What knits us together as Christians is not that we are homogenous people, but that we are *His* people. Not that we all agree but that we all believe.

ALICIA BRITT CHOLE
Pure Joy

❧

I do not pray for these alone, but also
for those who will believe in Me
through their word; that they all may be one.
JOHN 17:20

Life throws us curves all the time. And forks in the road. And roadblocks. In those times, we turn to the Lord for direction. And in His time, in His way, He gives it.

God's guidance shows the way that leads to true life. It is always for our good. And it will always come when we need it most.

PETER WALLACE
What the Psalmist Is Saying

✣

I praise you, LORD, for being my guide.
PSALM 16:7, CEV

The New Testament Greek word for *repent* means to stop traveling in one direction and turn 180 degrees around. While this New Testament word also communicates that one should feel sorrow and regret for his or her sin, the stress is on turning around and traveling back. Repentance is returning to God in whose likeness we are created. To repent is to begin the journey homeward.

HARRIET CROSBY
A Place Called Home

God did not send His Son into the world
to condemn the world, but that
the world through Him might be saved.

JOHN 3:17

Halo my path
with gentleness and love.

—PURITAN PRAYER

July 1

The psalms run the gamut from the deepest pain to the most ecstatic joy; and the key to it all is the fact that the psalmists always admit honestly just how they feel. But they don't make their feelings the center of their experience. No matter how much they've been abused, misunderstood, and hurt, no matter how much danger they're in or how many burdens they carry, the writers focus on God and not on themselves.

WARREN W. WIERSBE
The 20 Essential Qualities

~

My heart is overflowing
with a good theme; ...
my tongue is the pen of a ready writer.
PSALM 45:1

I love the sea. . . . I love to see the vast expanse of sky and water. I love to hear the waves crashing on the shore. I love to walk along the beach and feel the sand beneath my feet and the breeze blowing gently in my face. But the sea separates families and friends and entire continents from each other! In Heaven, there will be *nothing* to separate us from each other or from God. Ever!

ANNE GRAHAM LOTZ
Heaven: My Father's House

ॐ

Neither death nor life . . . nor things present nor things to come, . . . shall be able to separate us from the love of God.
ROMANS 8:38–39

an you imagine the outcome if a parent honored each request of each child during a trip? We'd inch our bloated bellies from one ice-cream store to the next. . . .

Can you imagine the chaos if God indulged each of ours?

MAX LUCADO
In the Eye of the Storm

᠅

I will give you a new heart
and put a new spirit within you.

EZEKIEL 36:26

Often people ask, "Isn't it selfish to pray about the petty details of everyday living?"

No, not if we take Jesus' word on this. The total stream of our lives is made of the sum of just such details. When we ask for God's help only in the major decisions, we are admitting Him into a very small part of our lives.

CATHERINE MARSHALL
Moments that Matter

᠅

Let my prayer come before You;
incline Your ear to my cry.
PSALM 88:2

July 5

Through the howling winds, Peter left the quaking boat and walked on water toward Jesus. Then fear attached itself like an anchor to his heart and he began to sink. Catching him, Jesus said, "O you of little faith, why did you doubt?" (Matt.14:31)

"Little faith." Though spoken to Peter, the other disciples knew the rebuke applied even more to them: at least Peter had the courage to get out of the boat.

ALICIA BRITT CHOLE
Pure Joy

❧

*The LORD is my light and
my salvation; whom shall I fear?*

PSALM 27:1

All masterpieces of painting contain both light and shadow. By them the artist highlights certain features of the subject, and they provide contrast and harmony to reveal beauty or character.

A happy life is not one filled only with sunshine, but one that uses *both* light and shadow to produce beauty.

BILLY GRAHAM
Unto the Hills

ༀ

*If you should suffer
for what is right, you are blessed.*
1 PETER 3:14, NIV

Jesus said that He came into our world for the specific purpose of giving us life—more abundant life. He is not the God of the tomb, but of resurrection morning. Give your life and your problems over to Him. I can guarantee that He has an answer tailor-made for *your* needs by One who loves you personally and wants to see you laugh again.

CATHERINE MARSHALL
Moments that Matter

&

*I have come that they may have life,
and that they may have it more abundantly.*
JOHN 10:10

Od isn't going to let you see the distant scene. So you might as well quit looking for it. He promises a lamp unto our feet, not a crystal ball into the future. We do not need to know what will happen tomorrow. We only need to know He leads us and we will find grace to help us when we need it.

MAX LUCADO
Traveling Light

రు

*Your word is a lamp
to my feet and a light to my path.*

PSALM 119:105

209

God loves each and every person who has ever been born into the human race! God loves the Eskimo living in an ice hut, the Chinese living in a bamboo lodge, . . . the royals living in a palace, . . . the peasant living in a farmhouse, . . . the slum dweller living in a housing project . . . the beggar with no housing at all.

God loves the whole world! God loves you! And God loves me!

ANNE GRAHAM LOTZ
God's Story

ↄ

*We have known and
believed the love that God has for us.*

1 JOHN 4:16

Our God is a compassionate God. His ear is always inclined toward our hearts. He listens with understanding and long-suffering. He does not grow deaf to our cries or turn away from our repetitious pleas. He loves to rejoice with us in our victories and mercifully hears our confession. Even more than we long to be heard, He desires to listen.

ANGELA THOMAS
Do You Think I'm Beautiful?

ℳ

Before they call I will answer;
while they are still speaking I will hear.

ISAIAH 65:24, NIV

July 11

We hope for good things that we cannot be sure of getting. Not being sure, we tend to worry. But we should not worry too much about worry; it comes with being spirits who can imagine the future and cannot control it. The trick is to develop a strong enough faith to keep worry in its place and then use worry to make us wise and careful in our hoping.

LEWIS SMEDES
Keeping Hope Alive

༄

*Blessed is the [person] who trusts
in the LORD, and whose hope is the LORD.*
JEREMIAH 17:7

For a child, there is no place quite so safe and secure as within the father's arms. Jesus invites you and me, in His name, to come into His Father's presence through prayer, crawl up into His lap by faith, put our head on His shoulder of strength, feel His loving arms of protection around us, call Him "Abba" Daddy, and pour out our hearts to Him.

ANNE GRAHAM LOTZ
My Heart's Cry

෨

*You received the Spirit of adoption
by whom we cry out, "Abba, Father."*
ROMANS 8:15

There is no such thing as an inferior prayer. Awkward prayers, tongue-tied prayers, prayers from a dry well, prayers from a giddy heart, even show-off prayers all have validity, not because of the one who is praying but because of the One who is listening. The thing is to keep talking, and when you run out of words, sit tight on a rock and listen. Just don't walk away.

LESLIE WILLIAMS
Night Wrestling

᠅

Whatever things you ask
in prayer, believing, you will receive.
MATTHEW 21:22

July 14

Christ gave His life to free us from every kind of sin.

When we are truly born again, our natural desires change. God forgives us and then changes our nature with the words, *Go and sin no more*. It is not a prerequisite for forgiveness, . . . forgiveness has already been extended. It is a vote of confidence.

LISA BEVERE
Kissed the Girls

༈

[He] gave Himself for us, that He might redeem us from every lawless deed and purify for Himself His own special people.
TITUS 2:14

The blessing God wants to pour out on your life and mine is not necessarily increased wealth or problem-free health or material prosperity. And it is not obtainable by prayerfully reciting a formula as though you are rubbing Aladdin's lamp, waiting for the Divine Genie to pop out and grant your request. The fullness of the blessing God wants to give you and me can be summed up in one word—*Jesus!*

ANNE GRAHAM LOTZ
My Heart's Cry

॰ঌ

God . . . has blessed us
with every spiritual blessing
in the heavenly places in Christ.

EPHESIANS 1:3

Levi is a Jew collecting taxes for the Romans and that makes him a traitor to his own people. But Levi is tough as nails. As a social and religious outcast, he has had to develop a thick skin over the years in order to survive. Yet Jesus takes one look at him, says a couple of words, and Levi simply drops everything to follow Him. What happened? Levi fell in love. . . . In an instant, Levi saw in Jesus' eyes a love both deep and vast.

HARRIET CROSBY
A Place Called Home

꽃

*Looking unto Jesus,
the author and finisher of our faith.*
HEBREWS 12:2

Our culture seems to demand focus on materiality, while our souls are starving. Just getting along from day to day, we seem to become covered with the pitch of the world, and like tar, materialism is difficult to get rid of. We walk around getting stuck to things that are not important to our salvation.

LESLIE WILLIAMS
Night Wrestling

❧

*You crown the year with Your goodness,
and Your paths drip with abundance.*

PSALM 65:11

G od allows us to have disappointments, frustrations, or even worse because He wants us to see that our joy is not in such worldly pleasures as success or money or popularity or health or sex or even in a miracle-working faith. Our joy is in the fact that we have a relationship with God. Few of us ever understand that message until circumstances have divested us of any possibility of help except by God Himself.

CATHERINE MARSHALL
Moments that Matter

∽

He . . . made us alive together with Christ.
EPHESIANS 2:4–5

July 19

I t is a waste of time trying to unscrew the inscrutable workings of God. You'll never be able to do it. That's simply the way God works. He honors faith and obedience. He will honor your faith if you will trust Him in a walk of obedience. And when you trust Him completely, you will enjoy inner quietness and security.

CHARLES SWINDOLL
Perfect Trust

ॐ

Let all those rejoice
who put their trust in You.

PSALM 5:11

There are certain things you can do that no one else can. Perhaps it is parenting, or constructing houses, or encouraging the discouraged. There are things that *only* you can do, and you are alive to do them. In the great orchestra we call life, you have an instrument and a song, and you owe it to God to play them both sublimely.

MAX LUCADO
The Applause of Heaven

*From My mother's womb
You have been My God.*
PSALM 22:10

221

Don't confuse happiness with joy. Happiness comes with happy circumstances; joy wells up deep inside our souls as we learn to trust Christ. Joy does not mean that we are never sad or that we never cry. But joy is a quiet confidence, a state of inner peace that comes from God.

Life's troubles will rob us of happiness. But they can never rob of God's joy.

BILLY GRAHAM
Unto the Hills

The joy of the LORD is your strength.

NEHEMIAH 8:10

You and I must place our faith in the God of Creation, Who is active in big ways, small ways, and unseen ways. Sometimes God tests and strengthens our faith by withholding evidence of His activity from us so that our faith is in Him alone. The men and women of God in the Old Testament were commended for faith that "is being sure of what we hope for and certain of what we do not see."

ANNE GRAHAM LOTZ
God's Story

※

*Faith is being sure of what
we hope for and
certain of what we do not see.*

HEBREWS 11:1, NIV

God created us as unique beings, and what's even more exciting than being an individual work of art is that God wants to spend time with us. He allows us to be lonely so we will seek Him, and He misses us when we avoid Him by packing the suitcases of our lives with stuff we can't take with us.

LESLIE WILLIAMS
Night Wrestling

*Your Father knows the things
you have need of before you ask Him.*

MATTHEW 6:8

What is it about the Bible that catches us off guard? That reaches into the depths of our souls and little by little begins to straighten us out? It digs up our arrogance and pride and enables us to forgive and forget. It creates spaces for understanding that we would not have thought possible. . . . Nothing of humankind can do that for us. Only God's Spirit has the ability to reach that deep into life.

LUCI SWINDOLL
I Married Adventure

❧

Oh, how I love Your law!
It is my meditation all the day.
PSALM 119:97

I n difficult times God expects that we shall simply settle down quietly upon the shore of His great grace and wait patiently for Him. He does not call us to beat our way with flashing wings and spent bodies against the storms of life.

He simply tells us that those who wait upon the Lord will mount up on wings refreshed.

W. PHILLIP KELLER
Sea Edge

ॐ

Those who wait on the LORD shall renew
their strength; they shall
mount up with wings like eagles.
ISAIAH 40:31

I n the midst of the swirling, cloying fog of fear, Jesus commands, "Stop it!" Stop letting your imagination run wild. Stop analyzing every detail over and over again. Stop flogging yourself with the "if only's" and "what if's."

How in the world is it possible to obey a command that involves so much of our emotional feelings? Our obedience begins with a choice to stop being afraid, followed by a decision to start trusting God.

ANNE GRAHAM LOTZ
My Heart's Cry

ॐ

Things work out when you trust in GOD.
PROVERBS 16:20, THE MESSAGE

The path to happiness is not found in selfish living and indifference to others. Instead, when we have experienced the mercy of God then we will show mercy to others. Then we will indeed be "twice blest" because we will both make others happy and experience true happiness ourselves.

BILLY GRAHAM
The Secret of Happiness

❧

You're blessed when you care.
MATTHEW 5:7, THE MESSAGE

The goal of parents is to see their children mature and free, able to handle the responsibilities of life and to contribute to the welfare of society. God's goal is for His children to use freedom responsibly for the good of others and the glory of the Lord.

WARREN W. WIERSBE
The 20 Essential Qualities

ॐ

[We] do not walk according to the flesh but according to the Spirit.

ROMANS 8:4

229

God loves to decorate. God *has* to decorate. Let Him live long enough in a heart, and that heart will begin to change. Portraits of hurt will be replaced by landscapes of grace. Walls of anger will be demolished and shaky foundations restored. God can no more leave a life unchanged than a mother can leave her child's tear untouched.

MAX LUCADO
Just Like Jesus

Your faithfulness reaches to the clouds.

PSALM 36:5

Because of His love for us, God sent His only Son to pay for every frivolous choice and every blatant sin and every dead-end path we have taken. . . . God treated Jesus as a sinner so that He can now treat us as righteous. It's almost unbelievable that because of Jesus' punishment, we can receive God's great affection. Because of Christ's obedience, we are the objects of God's great delight.

ANGELA THOMAS
Do You Think I'm Beautiful?

༈

God did not send His Son into the
world to condemn the world,
but that the world . . . might be saved.
JOHN 3:17

Hand your dream over to God, and leave it in His keeping. There seem to be periods when the dream is like a seed that must be planted in the dark earth and left there to germinate. This is not a time of passiveness on our part. There are things we can and must do—fertilizing, watering, weeding—hard work and self-discipline.

But the growth of that seed, . . . that is God's part of the process.

CATHERINE MARSHALL
Moments that Matter

ॐ

*The LORD shall preserve
your going out and your coming in.*

PSALM 121:8

August

❧

Not only is God loving.

He is love itself.

—C. H. Spurgeon

N o matter what the circumstances, God always has the last word. *Always.* And it is a word of triumph. There is no death! What joy! For those of us still left on earth puzzling it out, ultimately, after weeping through the night, we notice that the shades lighten slowly, and sunlight eventually pours in, making the dust motes dance, and making the room habitable once again.

The peace of God passes understanding.

LESLIE WILLIAMS
Night Wrestling

ॐ

The peace of God,
which surpasses all understanding,
will guard your hearts and minds.

PHILIPPIANS 4:7

When your world caves in. When the lights go out. When devastating news arrives. When fools rush in. When you have done everything you can and find yourself crushed by the weight of doing— right there is where God wants you to stop and be stilled. Stand before the only hope you have and wait.

ANGELA THOMAS
Do You Think I'm Beautiful?

Be still, and know that I am God.
PSALM 46:10

235

August 3

We are patterned after our heavenly Father, who uses His words to create and give life. This means we must choose to bless others with our words rather than curse them. We are called to be perfect as He is perfect. . . . The key is found in our speech. By bridling our tongue we control our whole being and may bring it under subjection to His Word of Truth.

LISA BEVERE
Be Angry but Don't Blow It!

ঽ

*The tongue
has the power of life
and death.*
PROVERBS 18:21, NIV

When we thoughtfully consider the world around us, we instinctively know our environment is not some haphazard cosmic accident but the handiwork of a Master Designer. The earth did not come about by the snap of some giant fingers but was deliberately planned and prepared. . . . Like Planet Earth around us, our lives are not a haphazard cosmos, either. They were deliberately planned to be filled with the beauty of love and joy and peace and purpose—with God Himself.

ANNE GRAHAM LOTZ
God's Story

🙢

The earth is the LORD's,
and all its fulness.
PSALM 24:1

August 5

Y ou hear the word *support* a lot today.
We all need support. And each of us
should be free to ask for and offer support
whenever needed.

But as the psalmist reminds us, the Lord
is our primary support. He holds us up. He
keeps us from failing under stress. He gives
us courage and power when we allow
ourselves to receive them.

PETER WALLACE
What the Psalmist Is Saying

کرک

*The LORD was my support. . . .
He delivered me because He delighted in me.*

PSALM 18:18–19

238

One day two Galileans, Simon and Andrew, were fishing. Jesus came by and said, "Follow me." The two fishermen dropped all caution. Common sense was put aside. They actually left their nets and their business opportunities and followed the Master. It was a sort of divine madness.

But the madness turned out to be wisdom; the Stranger became their Friend, their Lord.

CATHERINE MARSHALL
Moments that Matter

*If your heart is wise,
my heart will rejoice.*
PROVERBS 23:15

August 7

Anxiety feeds on life's complications, on striving to meet expectations, on perfectly following rules and regulations, on meeting deadlines, on doing more and more and more and more. But to live, to really *live*, in Christ requires only one thing—to love with abandon and no thought for tomorrow; to love regardless of whatever anxious times we may be living through; to love as though our lives depended on it.

HARRIET CROSBY
A Place Called Home

࠲

*Beloved, if God so loved us,
we also ought to love one another.*
1 JOHN 4:11

240

God is not a vending machine for
Christians, dispensing what we think
we need. The Christian journey is instead
the process of learning to accept Christ's
outstretched hand as He leads us down the
sometimes mucky road of life. We may be
covered with slosh from struggling along—
but once we get to the top of the hill, the
vistas are breathtaking.

LESLIE WILLIAMS
Night Wrestling

❧

You are my strong refuge.
Let my mouth be filled with Your praise.

PSALM 71:7–8

We wear Jesus. And those who don't believe in Jesus note that we do. They make decisions about Christ by watching us. When we are kind, they assume Christ is kind. When we are gracious, they assume Christ is gracious. But if we are brash, what will people think about our King? When we are dishonest, what assumptions will an observer make about our Master? . . . Courteous conduct honors Christ.

MAX LUCADO
A Love Worth Giving

ꙮ

All of you who were baptized into Christ have clothed yourselves with Christ.

GALATIANS 3:27, NIV

God doesn't need an abundance of words. He doesn't need a dissertation about your life. He just wants your attention. He wants your heart.

KATHY TROCCOLI
Hope for a Woman's Heart

ॐ

Draw near to God and
He will draw near to you

JAMES 4:8

Next time you feel afraid, make a list—not of your fears but of the characteristics of God. Find a Scripture . . . to substantiate each one as you reconsider your situation in light of Who God is. Then, if you feel it would be helpful to list your fears, make sure beside each one you write down the attribute of God that applies. The secret to peace lies in your focus. Plant your faith in Someone Who is bigger than your fears.

ANNE GRAHAM LOTZ
My Heart's Cry

∽

*Stand still and consider
the wondrous works of God.*

JOB 37:14

The most important thing we ever hope for from God is God Himself. Hope that He will be with us in our troubles. Not necessarily for Him to take our troubles away, but always to be there: under us to hold us up, ahead of us to lead the way, behind us to push us along, over us to keep an eye on us, and in us to keep alive our hopes of getting beyond our troubles.

LEWIS SMEDES
Keeping Hope Alive

*You are my hiding place
and my shield;
I hope in Your word.*
PSALM 119:114

August 13

S haring ourselves with others is much more than a responsibility or even a privilege; it's a grace. Grace means that God does something in and through us for His glory, not that we do something for God and get credit for it.

Grace living begins when we give ourselves to the Lord and to others.

WARREN W. WIERSBE
The 20 Essential Qualities

∽

*They first gave themselves to the Lord,
and then to us by the will of God.*

2 CORINTHIANS 8:5

The death of the seed that falls into the ground produces a new cycle of life—the fresh little shoot, the full stalk, the bud, the flower. . . . The fruit dies to allow the seed to fall once again into the ground. The seed dies and there is a new beginning. Nothing is ever wasted. In God's economy, whether He is making a flower or a human soul, nothing ever comes to nothing.

ELISABETH ELLIOT
The Path of Loneliness

و

Because Your lovingkindness is
better than life, my lips shall praise You.
PSALM 63:3

Life is hard; no doubt about it. But in it there's lots of depth to be explored and growth to be experienced. That's all part of the adventure. For me personally, exploring, knowing, and experiencing starts and ends with the fact that Jesus loves me. He tells me so. And it is that divine love that transforms the human heart.

LUCI SWINDOLL
I Married Adventure

⁓

Blessed be the LORD your God,
who delighted in you.

1 KINGS 10:9

Need is a voice that never says,
"Enough!" Yet Jesus was not a slave
to that voice. What was His secret? Jesus' aim
was doing His Father's will and finishing His
Father's work. That focus placed the world's
demands in proper perspective.

ALICIA BRITT CHOLE
Pure Joy

ᔓ

*Whoever desires to come
after Me, let him deny himself.*
MARK 8:34

Y ou can talk to God because God listens. Your voice matters in heaven. He takes you very seriously. When you enter His presence, the attendants turn to you to hear your voice. No need to fear that you will be ignored. Even if you stammer or stumble, even if what you have to say impresses no one, it impresses God, and He listens.

MAX LUCADO
The Great House of God

*I cry out to the LORD;
I pray to
the LORD for mercy.*
PSALM 142:1, NCV

August 18

God's Word encourages us to speak words of encouragement, support, and praise. To build up rather than tear down. To confront when necessary, but with strength and love balanced. To tell the truth about a situation, about our feelings, and about life in general.

PETER WALLACE
What the Psalmist Is Saying

⁓

Let my words and my thoughts
be pleasing to you, LORD, because
you are my mighty rock and my protector.
PSALM 19:14, CEV

251

It is under the shaping, chiseling forces of life's varied experiences that Christ can sculpt us into magnificent masterpieces.... These are the well-worn tools of His trade for turning out beautiful souls. His Spirit can work wonders on the rough stone of our tough wills, bringing them into lovely conformity to His own will.

It is this sort of person, who, standing tall, despite the worst weather, reflects back something of the warmth and wholesomeness of Christ.

W. PHILLIP KELLER
Sea Edge

The LORD has been mindful of us;
He will bless us.

PSALM 115:12

Jesus paid dearly for the gift of peace, hanging on the cross for us sinners. We don't deserve peace at all; rather, we deserve the trials we inflict on ourselves and others through our sin and ignorance. However, God paid so we could share in the gift of peace, and part of our gratitude is remembering the cost of Jesus' suffering.

LESLIE WILLIAMS
Night Wrestling

~

The LORD will give strength to His people;
the LORD will bless His people with peace.

PSALM 29:11

Rejections are like speed bumps on the road. They come with the journey.... You can't keep people from rejecting you. But you can keep rejections from enraging you. How? By letting God's acceptance compensate for their rejection.

When others reject you, let God accept you. He is not frowning. He is not mad. He sings over you. Take a long drink from His limitless love.

MAX LUCADO
A Love Worth Giving

∽

God is my salvation and
my glory; the rock of my strength.

PSALM 62:7

I have learned that if I don't give access to
the truths of God to enter my heart,
many other "voices" will get my attention.
Especially in times of crisis.

The invitation is always open to
commune with God. No matter what.

KATHY TROCCOLI
Hope for a Woman's Heart

*May You hear the supplication
of Your servant . . .
and when You hear, forgive.*

1 KINGS 8:30

255

Through it *all*. That's the ticket. Through the victories and the failures.... Through the brilliant days of accomplishment and the broken days.... Through the heady days of laughter and success and those nameless intervals of setback and blank despair. Through it all, God is with us, leading us, teaching us, humbling us, preparing us.

CHARLES SWINDOLL
Moses: A Man of Selfless Dedication

৵

He is my refuge and my fortress:
my God; in Him I will trust.

PSALM 91:2

Just as surely as God implants the life cell in the tiny seed that produces the mighty oak . . . as surely as He instills the heartbeat in the life of the tiny infant yet unborn . . . as surely as He puts motion into the planets, stars, and heavenly bodies—so He implants His divine life in the hearts of men who earnestly seek Him through Christ.

BILLY GRAHAM
Unto the Hills

᳁

Unless one is born again,
he cannot see
the kingdom of God.
JOHN 3:3

The answer to our loneliness is love—not our finding someone to love us, but our surrendering to the God who has always loved us with an everlasting love. Loving Him is then expressed in a happy and full-hearted pouring out of ourselves in love to others.

ELISABETH ELLIOT
The Path of Loneliness

Everyone who loves Him who begot also loves him who is begotten of Him.

1 JOHN 5:1

Jesus is the way, He does not have a way. He does not merely give us a map out of the labyrinthine maze of our confusion. He *is* the way. E. Stanley Jones found himself in a jungle where there was no path. His guide furiously hacked away through the dense underbrush, trying to clear a way. Jones said to his guide, "Are you sure this leads to the path?" The guide answered, "Bhanna, right now, I *am* your path." Jesus is our path, our way.

FAWN PARISH
It's All About You, Jesus

~

I am the way,
the truth, and the life.
JOHN 14:6

It doesn't matter if your life has been dry, barren, bleak, desolate, . . . or if it has become that way because of some tragedy or crisis. If you submit your life to the skillful touch of the Creator, He has the power to transform you into someone who is beautiful—beautiful not because of a toned physique or flawless skin or a perfect figure or manageable hair but because the life of Christ radiates from within.

ANNE GRAHAM LOTZ
God's Story

~

My heart trusted in Him, and I am helped;
therefore my heart greatly rejoices.

PSALM 28:7

We can love because God first loves us, making us feel safe. He is faithful, and we are all *first* on His list. This is not some fleeting, elementary-school crush. We have an assurance of His love because He loved us before we even glanced His way.

LISA BEVERE
Kissed the Girls

We love Him because He first loved us.
1 JOHN 4:19

August 29

_____

When kindness comes grudgingly,
we'll remember God's kindness to us
and ask Him to make us more kind. When
patience is scarce, we'll thank Him for His
and ask Him to make us more patient.
When it's hard to forgive, we won't list all
the times we've been given grief. Rather,
we'll list all the times we've been given
grace and pray to become more forgiving.

MAX LUCADO
A Love Worth Giving

ॐ

*My peace I give to you;
not as the world gives do I give to you.*
JOHN 14:27

The peace that passes understanding bypasses the heart's desire entirely, giving us not what we thought we wanted, but what God wanted us to have—which turns out to be better than anything our puny imaginations could concoct in the first place.

LESLIE WILLIAMS
Night Wrestling

*I will heal them and reveal to them
the abundance of peace and truth.*
JEREMIAH 33:6

263

If we are not consumed with God, we will most definitely be consumed with other things. We were created to worship God and if we don't set our affections there, we will easily worship something or someone else.

KATHY TROCCOLI
Hope for a Woman's Heart

ɔ

*Set your minds
on things above not on earthly things.*

COLOSSIANS 3:2, NIV

September

Prayer is a path
where there is none.
—NOAH BENSHEA

It ought to comfort rather than upset us when our own arrangements go awry—especially if we have prayed for guidance and the accomplishment of the will of God. The disruption of our own plans is sometimes the very means of God's working out His own—not that we have disobeyed or ignored His directions, but that He may assure us of His serene Providence. Our lives are in *His* hands, not our own.

ELISABETH ELLIOT
The Music of His Promises

꙾

*The LORD works out everything
for His own ends.*
PROVERBS 16:4, NIV

The Hebrew word for salvation means to make wide, to make sufficient. Jesus is so spacious that Eugene Peterson says, "All of God fits within Him without crowding." We fit in Him as well, with all our brokenness, our frail egos, our thumb-sucking immaturity and coddled fears. We are in Him who is spacious with wholeness, health, and vitality.

FAWN PARISH
It's All About You, Jesus

*It is good that one should hope and
wait quietly for the salvation of the LORD.*
LAMENTATIONS 3:26

True peace is like seeing Christ face to face: an experience so moving, so awesome, so terrifying in a way that I'm not sure, on this earth, we can stand more than the fleeting glimpses we receive.

My experience, however, is that peace is worth praying for every minute of every day. The struggle is always worth it: God's peace makes holy our relationships with others, with ourselves, and with the Almighty.

LESLIE WILLIAMS
Night Wrestling

&

Having been justified by faith,
we have peace with God.
ROMANS 5:1

A great Scottish preacher once said: The most profane word we use is "hopeless." When you say a situation or a person is hopeless, you are slamming the door in the face of God.

Don't slam the door in the face of the One who offers you hope. Your circumstances are part of a much bigger plan.

KATHY TROCCOLI
Hope for a Woman's Heart

✄

Hope in God, for I shall yet
praise Him for the help of His countenance.

PSALM 42:5

September 5

How the heavenly Father must shake His head and smile ruefully at His children! We hold so tightly to things we can see and hear and taste and feel and smell right here and now, when all along, He is planning to give us things that "no eye has seen, no ear has heard. . . ." His blessings for us are going to be way beyond our wildest imaginations.

ANNE GRAHAM LOTZ
My Heart's Cry

❧

Eye has not seen, nor ear heard
. . . the things which God
has prepared for those who love Him.

1 CORINTHIANS 2:9

The Lord is high above every other living thing, seen and unseen. His strength is measureless and unfailing. He never tires. He never needs to rest.

That's the God you know and serve today. Strong, ready, and able to defend you and uphold you and pursue you. Above any trouble or pain you may feel. His power knows no bounds.

PETER WALLACE
What the Psalmist Is Saying

ॐ

Show your strength, LORD,
so that we may sing and praise your power.
PSALM 21:13, CEV

S alvation is intentionally quite impossible apart from Jesus. God has designed our moment-by-moment life to be impossible to live right without Jesus. Our everyday is just as important as our eternity. So Jesus is for us, right now, this very moment. There is no activity of your life outside the scope of His love and interest. There is no moment that He will not save you.

FAWN PARISH
It's All About You, Jesus

ᔥ

O LORD, be gracious to us. . . .
Be . . . our salvation
also in the time of trouble.
ISAIAH 33:2

God longs to wash us clean. He offers us the best if we will be first willing, and then obedient. Willing to repent and say we've gone astray. Willing to serve Him with joy because He is good, faithful, and true. Willing to submit in obedience to His Word, for it is the law of love, life, and liberty. Willing to take up our cross and hide our life in Christ, the Word made flesh, and follow His example.

LISA BEVERE
Kissed the Girls

*Though your sins are like scarlet,
they shall be as white as snow.*
ISAIAH 1:18

Westminster Abbey in London is a grand cathedral . . . where the kings and queens receive their coronation. The narthex is small, dark, and cramped—just a brief space to pass through between the outside door and the door leading into the cathedral itself. I can't imagine anyone visiting the abbey and being satisfied to stay in the narthex.

Your life and mine here on earth is like the narthex to a grand cathedral. Our lives are simply an area to pass through on our way to the glory of eternal life that lies beyond the door of death.

ANNE GRAHAM LOTZ
My Heart's Cry

My flesh . . . will rest in hope.

PSALM 16:9

Unless we genuinely love each other, unless we truly care for each other, unless we are living in harmony, *the world will not believe.*

Everybody wants the real deal. And when you show the real deal—the purity of love—it is hard to resist. There is no moving toward God without love. If we who bear His name do not love, Jesus tells us the world will dismiss *Him*.

DEE BRESTIN AND KATHY TROCCOLI
The Colors of His Love

❧

By this all will know that you are
My disciples, if you have love for one another.
JOHN 13:35

September 11

Those of us who wish to be utterly honest with ourselves and with our Father know full well the need of His covering. We cry from the depths: "Who can cover my iniquities? Who can enfold me in righteousness? Who can fill me with the fullness of God?"

It is He and only He who can do this for us.

W. PHILLIP KELLER
Sea Edge

৵

To the LORD our God belong
mercy and forgiveness,
though we have rebelled against Him.

DANIEL 9:9

Every time we feel tempted to find security in our finances or our belongings, we must fight the temptation. God brought us into the world naked, and He loves us whether we wear rags or designer clothes. God loves us, rich or poor.

LESLIE WILLIAMS
Seduction of the Lesser Gods

❧

Blessed is every one who fears
the LORD, who walks in His ways.

PSALM 128:1

277

We do not come to know God through works—we come to know Him by faith through grace. We cannot work our way toward happiness and heaven; we cannot moralize our way, we cannot reform our way, we cannot buy our way. Salvation comes as a gift of God through Christ.

BILLY GRAHAM
The Secret of Happiness

❧

Help me, O LORD my God!
Oh, save me according to Your mercy.
PSALM 109:26

When Jesus promised us "knock, and the door will be opened to you," it is implied that there is a time when the door remains shut. This period of activity on our part, with no seeming results, is the time when our faith often falters. But when faith persists, it is rewarded by an act of initiative on God's part. It is He who opens the door to our needs and solves our problems.

CATHERINE MARSHALL
Moments that Matter

ఌ

Knock, and it will be opened to you.

MATTHEW 7:7

The Lord your Shepherd invites you to His pasture to feed on satisfying greenery. To drink of the clear, clean water. To follow the path to fulfillment that He sets before you.

Your soul is well fed in the loving Shepherd's care.

PETER WALLACE
What the Psalmist Is Saying

ॐ

You lead me to streams of peaceful water,
and you refresh my life.
PSALM 23:2–3, CEV

When you find yourself in a forced stillness—waiting in line, sitting by a hospital bed, or stuck in traffic—instead of fidgeting and fuming, use such moments to practice stillness before God.

It's a crazy world and life speeds by at a blur, yet God is right in the middle of craziness. And anywhere, at anytime, we may turn to Him, hear His voice, feel His hand, and catch the fragrance of heaven.

JONI EARECKSON TADA
Holiness in Hidden Places

The LORD is at your right hand.

PSALM 110:5

When we hurt, when we fail, when we are frightened, God wants us to draw near . . . into His arms of safety and love.

God isn't aloof and unapproachable, but quickly comes to our aid and with His great might saves us. He doesn't reject or condemn us when we cry out in fear or helplessness. He delights in quieting His children just as any mother considers it a joy to comfort her own.

LISA BEVERE
Kissed the Girls

৵

As one whom his mother comforts,
so I will comfort you.

ISAIAH 66:13

Our precious Jesus will meet extra-ordinary pain with extraordinary grace.

He will meet extraordinary needs with extraordinary resources.

He will meet extraordinary fears with extraordinary comfort.

KATHY TROCCOLI
Hope for a Woman's Heart

❧

You will keep him in perfect peace,
whose mind is stayed
on You, because he trusts in You.

ISAIAH 26:3

283

A *gape* love cares for others because God has cared for us. *Agape* love goes beyond sentiment and good wishes. Because God loved first, *agape* love responds. Because God was gracious, *agape* love forgives the mistake when the offense is high. *Agape* offers patience when stress is abundant and extends kindness when kindness is rare. Why? Because God offered us both.

MAX LUCADO
A Love Worth Giving

⌇

Love suffers long and is kind.
1 CORINTHIANS 13:4

The whole idea that our lives belong to us is a myth, and an arrogant assumption when it comes right down to it. I did not conceive myself; I wasn't my own idea. I cannot will myself to wake up in the mornings—it is by God's grace alone that I am given even one more day to live.

LESLIE WILLIAMS
Night Wrestling

᳹

*And of His fullness we have
all received, and grace for grace.*

JOHN 1:16

285

The Greek word translated "workmanship" is *poiema*; it means "something made" and gives us the English word *poem*. The Christian who boasts, "I'm a self-made person!" doesn't understand this basic principle that God must work *in* us before He can work *through* us. He must prepare us for what He has prepared for us.

WARREN W. WIERSBE
The 20 Essential Qualities

We are His workmanship,
created in Christ Jesus for good works.
EPHESIANS 2:10

Hospitality is a grand gesture of acceptance. Christ's hospitality is forgiveness and acceptance. It welcomes friends and family, strangers and sinners. Because we live in Christ, the hospitality with which we welcome others is generated by a deep, passionate, single-minded love of Jesus extended to all comers. Hospitality comes from the heart, Christ's true home.

HARRIET CROSBY
A Place Called Home

❦

Love one another fervently with a pure heart.
1 PETER 1:22

I n God's eyes, there are no little people…
because there are no big people. We are
all on the same playing field. We all start at
square one. No one has it better than the
other, or possesses unfair advantage.

Success is not a key. Faithfulness is.

JONI EARECKSON TADA
Holiness in Hidden Places

჻

I will hope continually,
and will praise You yet more and more.
PSALM 71:14

L ove is an act of will: listening to someone when we are bored, keeping that perfectly couched comeback to ourselves, letting old Mrs. Jones win the argument over something unimportant, biting our tongues instead of reminding others of our triumphs.

Love is the decision to behave a certain way even when we don't feel like it.

LESLIE WILLIAMS
Seduction of the Lesser Gods

꙳

Love cares more for others than for self.
1 CORINTHIANS 13:4, *THE MESSAGE*

289

You have the ability, with your words, to make a person stronger. Your words are to their soul what a vitamin is to their body.

Do not withhold encouragement from the discouraged. Do not keep affirmation from the beaten down! Speak words that make people stronger. Believe in them as God has believed in you.

MAX LUCADO
A Love Worth Giving

✣

*When you talk, do not say harmful things,
but say what people need—
words that will help others become stronger.*

EPHESIANS 4:29, NCV

"I accept you as you are."

"I believe you are valuable."

"I care when you hurt."

"I desire only what is best for you."

"I erase all offenses."

We could call that the ABC's of love. And I don't know of anybody who would turn his back on such magnetic, encouraging statements.

CHARLES SWINDOLL
Dropping Your Guard

❦

All the law is fulfilled in one word; . . .
love your neighbor as yourself.

GALATIANS 5:14

291

God's definition of true beauty is not in terms of charm, charisma or the subtle flatteries of fashion. . . . It is, rather, beauty of behavior, loyalty of life, serenity of spirit.

He knows full well the best way to make me attractive to His eyes. No matter what storms, trials or stress are brought to bear upon my soul I shall see them as His tools for shaping my character into a winsome piece of His workmanship.

W. PHILLIP KELLER
Sea Edge

~

God is greater than our heart,
and knows all things.
1 JOHN 3:20

Hospitality is a grand gesture of grace. Living a hospitable life is a way of imitating Christ, the Gracious Host. When we practice hospitality, we practice grace. We accept people for exactly who they are, not for who we would like them to be. Practicing hospitality helps us to let go of that anxious need to control and graciously accept others just as they are.

HARRIET CROSBY
A Place Called Home

*In the house of the righteous
there is much treasure.*

PROVERBS 15:6

293

Only Christ can satisfy, whether we have or don't have, whether we are known or unknown, whether we live or die. . . . The pursuit of happiness is the cultivation of a Christ-centered, Christ-controlled life.

CHARLES SWINDOLL
Laugh Again

ॐ

The upright shall dwell in Your presence.
PSALM 140:13

The person who lives by faith trusts that good things can happen because God wants good things to happen and is able to make them happen. Even when the odds are against their happening. When they don't happen, she keeps on waiting for them to happen. And even if something bad should happen first, she expects something good to come of it later on.

LEWIS SMEDES
Keeping Hope Alive

༄

*Imitate those who through faith
and patience inherit the promises.*
HEBREWS 6:12

October

❧

God loves us as individuals.

He knows us by name.

—LUCILLE SOLLENBERGER

Holiness isn't in a style of dress. It's not a matter of rules and regulations. It's a way of life that emanates quietness and rest, joy in family, shared pleasure with friends, the help of a neighbor—and the hope of a Savior.

JONI EARECKSON TADA
Holiness in Hidden Places

*As the elect of God, . . . put on
tender mercies, kindness,
humility, meekness, longsuffering.*
COLOSSIANS 3:12

Economical is good, but too economical can become stingy. Orderly is good, but too orderly can mean rigid, with a loss of spontaneity.

Think not only of your gifts but also of ... the boundaries that God in His wisdom has set up in your life. Acknowledging and accepting our limitations are the keys to finding out who we really are rather than who we think we ought to be.

INGRID TROBISCH
The Confident Woman

Every good gift and
every perfect gift is from above.
JAMES 1:17

Prayer is Sabbath. No matter what the actual content of our prayers, in prayer God calls us to trust Him, to rest in Him. When we pray, we lay down our burdens before the throne of Grace. Whether we pray for ourselves or others, we put ourselves or those for whom we pray to rest in God's hands. We enter the Sabbath.

HARRIET CROSBY
A Place Called Home

∽

Pray without ceasing.

1 THESSALONIANS 5:17

In the process of spiritual development, we are tempted to view prayers answered "yes" as an affirmation of God's love, not realizing that prayer is answered "yes," or "no," or "maybe," or "not yet," or with total silence—and that God loves us no matter what the answer is.

LESLIE WILLIAMS
Night Wrestling

The eyes of the LORD are on the righteous,
and His ears are open to their prayers.

1 PETER 3:12

G od's Word is not merely letters on paper . . . it's *alive*. . . . It is so sharp it can separate the soul from the spirit, and in the process, reveal our hidden thoughts and attitudes.

Remember nothing (no thing) is hidden from God. He sees it all, but we do not. Often our very own hearts deceive us, but if we ask for truth, God will share His discernment with us through His word.

LISA BEVERE
Kissed the Girls

&

The word of God is living and powerful, . . .
piercing even to the
division of soul and spirit.
HEBREWS 4:12

Believers are not optimists, they are people of hope. Their only reason for so huge a hope is the story of how the Maker of the world once came to His world, died, lived again, and still intends to come back and fix His world once for all.

LEWIS SMEDES
Keeping Hope Alive

*I have set the LORD always before me;
because He is at my right
hand I shall not be moved.*

PSALM 16:8

God has paid a great price to make His grace available to us. For us to deliberately go our own way and live only to please ourselves is to receive His grace in vain. It means putting a cheap price tag on the cross of Christ.

WARREN W. WIERSBE
The 20 Essential Qualities

᙭

We . . . plead with you
not to receive the grace of God in vain.

2 CORINTHIANS 6:1

We know vacations lift our spirits, that the first daffodils pushing up through the frozen earth gladden our hearts, and a newborn baby puts a smile on everyone's face. But have we ever experienced a continuous *full* feeling of joy?

Living in *complete* joy requires living in *complete confidence* in God. . . . Our joy is inextinguishable when we completely trust His heart.

DEE BRESTIN AND KATHY TROCCOLI
The Colors of His Love

მ

In Your presence is fullness of joy.
PSALM 16:11

October 9

If we are to love people as Christ commanded us, then we must be willing not to plant our feet on our side of the fence, howling self-righteous epithets to the other side, but rather to climb over the fence and see what the world looks like from the other point of view.

LESLIE WILLIAMS
Seduction of the Lesser Gods

⌘

Love . . . puts up with anything, . . .
always looks for the best.

1 CORINTHIANS 13:6–7, *THE MESSAGE*

Praying to make a difference in this world means we learn to get past ourselves and our problems and pursue a greater purpose. It's not that God doesn't want us to come to Him with our needs. He just doesn't want us to *stop* there.

JOHN HULL AND TIM ELMORE
Pivotal Praying

᠉

How great is Your goodness, . . . which You have prepared for those who trust in You.
PSALM 31:19

I f Jesus, with His continual awareness of the Father's luminous presence and guidance could do or say nothing without His Father, then how much greater is our need for Him? . . .

What this means is that each day I must find a way to walk with Him, talk with Him. And not just during my morning prayer time, but during the entire day.

CATHERINE MARSHALL
Moments that Matter

❧

The Son can do nothing of His own accord.

JOHN 5:19, RSV

It's amazing how you can get carried away from worries and woes and self-concern when you start naming out loud what you're thankful for. Right away your focus shifts from your needs to the Father's graciousness and love.

Try it!

CHARLES SWINDOLL
Day by Day

࠾

Let us come before
His presence with thanksgiving.
PSALM 95:2

Fear keeps us from risking and reaching out. Fear prevents us from asking forgiveness of those we have hurt. Fear hinders us from asking for the support we need from a friend. Fear keeps us cowering from our tough circumstances instead of standing up in God's power, facing them, and working through them.

But as a child of God, you have a source of power and strength: the Lord Himself.

PETER WALLACE
What the Psalmist Is Saying

෯

You, LORD, . . . protect me,
and I have no fears.
PSALM 27:1, CEV

Time and time again, we live our lives governed by a pressing list of things to do. More than anything else, urgency keeps our lives in chains, keeps our stomachs in knots, keeps our hearts fluttering erratically—and keeps our souls at a shouting distance, instead of a whispering distance, from God. Most of us need reminding that eternity is not measured with a stopwatch.

LESLIE WILLIAMS
Seduction of the Lesser Gods

∾

I will be their God, and
they shall be My people.
2 CORINTHIANS 6:16

Though there's a majestic and powerful beauty on the surface of the ocean, there's even more beauty when you dive beneath the waves—luxuriant seaweed swaying gracefully . . . , small fish darting here and there, . . . a world that's quiet and deep.

When you dive beneath the surface things of God, you also discover an endless calm—a world of divine life that is quiet and deep. There, in the depths, God will reveal a quiet and gentle kind of interior beauty.

JONI EARECKSON TADA
Holiness in Hidden Places

*In quietness and
confidence shall be your strength.*
ISAIAH 30:15

J esus always knocks before entering.
He doesn't have to. He owns your heart.

   If anyone has the right to barge in,
Christ does.

   But He doesn't.

   That gentle tap you here? It's Christ.

MAX LUCADO
A Love Worth Giving

Behold, I stand at the door and knock.

REVELATION 3:20

The only attachment of the word *holy* in the Ten Commandments is to the word *Sabbath*. God makes something out of nothing, hangs the universe, forms myriad creatures out of His fertile imagination. After finishing all that He takes a rest when He is not tired. By resting, He makes *time* holy. He has just made a whole universe of things, very impressive things mind you. . . . But His final touch, His most unexpected behavior, is rest. God makes time sacred by declaring the Sabbath day holy.

FAWN PARISH
It's All About You, Jesus

~

Remember the Sabbath day, to keep it holy.
EXODUS 20:8

It's the hilarious giver, the extravagant giver, who gets the blessing. When we start to calculate how much we can afford to do or to give, we stop living by faith and depending on grace. Of course, we should not be careless and wasteful, although my idea of wastefulness might be God's idea of generosity.

WARREN W. WIERSBE
The 20 Essential Qualities

The generous soul will be made rich.

PROVERBS 11:25

315

Somehow, I don't think God is impressed with a single item on the conventional resume I have worked up for job applications.

Rather than citing our degrees, honors, and awards, we'd probably make Him happiest by working on love, joy, peace, patience, kindness, goodness, faithfulness, gentleness, and self-control.

LESLIE WILLIAMS
Seduction of the Lesser Gods

૪

*When we live God's way . . . He brings gifts
into our lives, . . . —things like
affections for others,
exuberance about life, serenity.*
GALATIANS 5:22, THE MESSAGE

People who depend on circumstances and other people for the strength they need to keep going will constantly be frustrated and worried, like a pilot flying a plane whose fuel tank is empty and there is no place to land for refueling. But people who depend on Jesus Christ to energize and motivate the inner person have the adequacy they need for every circumstance of life.

WARREN W. WIERSBE
The 20 Essential Qualities

᠄ᢒ

God is able to make all grace
abound toward you,
that you . . . may have
an abundance for every good work.

2 CORINTHIAN 9:8

God's goal is not necessarily to make us happy. His goal is to make us His.

There are thousands of times when we'll ask God what He is doing to us. We must be more concerned with what He wants to do *in* us. I am talking about conforming us into the image of Christ. And only the Lord knows what it will take to conform us into the image of His son.

KATHY TROCCOLI
Hope for a Woman's Heart

❧

Whom the LORD loves He corrects.

PROVERBS 3:12

Do you feel overwhelmed and smothered by pressure? Are you desperate for "breathing room"? Do you try to escape the stress through an extended vacation, therapeutic counseling, . . . or entertainment, . . . only to find . . . you are no better than you were before, because the pressure is from within?

Only God has the power to lift the pressure from within you. . . . He can give your spirit peace and rest.

ANNE GRAHAM LOTZ
God's Story

☙

*The righteous shall be glad
in the LORD, and trust in Him.*

PSALM 64:10

If I choose to live out of my emotions, no telling what might happen or where I might go to salve my depression, dissatisfaction, or discouragement. Feelings fluctuate with the day, the wind, my hormones, circumstances, and human relationships. But because God told me He doesn't change, I can choose to believe Him no matter how I feel. This is … living out of doctrine rather than feelings.

LUCI SWINDOLL
I Married Adventure

❧

I am the LORD, I do not change.

MALACHI 3:6

The Eastern shepherd of Jesus' day raised his sheep primarily in the Judean uplands. The countryside was rocky, hilly, and creased with deep crevices and ravines. So the shepherd had to establish a personal relationship with each sheep. He knew their names, and when he called them, they recognized his voice. The Bible describes our relationship with Jesus as being similar to the Eastern shepherd and his sheep— a relationship based on His voice. And make no mistake about it, His voice is God's Word.

ANNE GRAHAM LOTZ
My Heart's Cry

I will not forget Your word.
PSALM 119:16

G od made us human *beings,* not human *doings.* The feeling associated with urgency—increased heart rate, pumping adrenaline, TMJ, headaches, tight muscles, the tendency to drive too fast, to talk too much, to speed from one activity to another —rob us of the great pleasures of peace, serenity, and quietude so necessary for an enriched relationship with God.

LESLIE WILLIAMS
Seduction of the Lesser Gods

*He has made His wonderful works
to be remembered; the LORD
is gracious and full of compassion.*

PSALM 111:4

God is the captain of our ship as we sail through storm-tossed seas. His Word in the lighthouse, to protect us from the hidden rocks beneath the dark waters. Ignoring the light-house, or "grabbing" the wheel from His capable hands, will lead to destruction.

He knows what is right for us. Let's let Him get us home.

KATHY TROCCOLI
Hope for a Woman's Heart

~

*May the Lord direct your hearts into
the love of God and into the patience of Christ.*

2 THESSALONIANS 3:5

I am drawn to God by the irresistible magnetism of His own greatness. There are pensive moments when in awe and wonder I sense that at best I can only experience "the edge of His life." There is a dimension, at least in my earth life, in which He will never be known in all His magnificence. With my human fallibility and spiritual limitations I shall never fully comprehend the length or depth or breadth of His infinite, amazing love.

W. PHILLIP KELLER
Sea Edge

❧

They shall sing of the ways of the LORD,
for great is the glory of the LORD.
PSALM 138:5

The most significant decision I can make on a day-to-day basis is my choice of attitude. It is more important than my past, my education, my bankroll, my successes or failures, fame or pain, what other people think of me or say about me, my circumstances, or my position. When my attitudes are right, there's no barrier too high, no valley too deep, no dream too extreme, no challenge too great.

CHARLES SWINDOLL
Strengthening Your Grip

*Be imitators of
God as dear children.*

EPHESIANS 5:1

God is continually after our hearts. Our hearts need to be broken by the things that break the heart of God. Without this work in us we will maneuver ourselves through life with our opinions, our judgments, and our summations. God knows that to build up our faith we need to grow continually in knowledge of Him.

KATHY TROCCOLI
Hope for a Woman's Heart

The knowledge of the truth leads to godliness.
TITUS 1:1, NIV

S wings make us feel weightless—for a few
  moments we defy the laws of gravity. For
a few moments we fly.

Dreams do much the same thing. As we
dream we press past the confines of what is
and what has been. As our minds dare to
see the unseen, our imagination fuels
our faith and we begin to trust God for
something more.

ALICIA BRITT CHOLE
Pure Joy

ॐ

*May the God of hope fill you with
all joy and peace in believing,
that you may abound
in hope by the power of the Holy Spirit.*

ROMANS 15:13

As long as the future is the future, it remains out of reach. It's only as the future crests into the present that we have any real power over it, or that it has any real power over us. We give the future too much power when we project our current fears, hopes, and dreams into the abstraction of what's to come. Here and now is all we've got.

LESLIE WILLIAMS
Night Wrestling

ॐ

Cause me to know the way in which
I should walk, for I lift up my soul to You.
PSALM 143:8

November

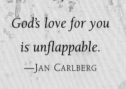

God's love for you is unflappable.

—Jan Carlberg

God calls us to be active in others' lives; He also calls us to be alone. The balance between community and solitude is a delicate one, because both are necessary for our spiritual well-being. When we wander too far in either direction, our lives get out of kilter.

LESLIE WILLIAMS
Night Wrestling

❧

Lead me in Your truth and teach me,
for You are the God of my salvation.
PSALM 25:5

God provides. Whether we fear He won't, or whether we feel certain He will, God pulls us through the tight places. The choice is ours—to live in fear or in trust.

True security is not in the bank, but in the assurance that God will take care of us.

W. PHILLIP KELLER
Sea Edge

ॐ

*The Lord is faithful, who will
establish you and guard you from the evil one.*
2 THESSALONIANS 3:3

November 3

We look for . . . joy in our careers, in money, in power, in all sorts of material things. But if they really brought lasting joy, wouldn't we have testimonies from millions of people around the world to that effect?

Try putting Christ first and watch how your life is turned around. You will discover where the love, peace, joy, and acceptance you've been searching for is to be found.

BILLY GRAHAM
Unto the Hills

౨

I will love You, O LORD, my strength.

PSALM 18:1

God's presence comes to dwell in our midst when we praise Him, and in His presence we find healing, transformation, and direction for our lives. In fact, the more time we spend praising the Lord, the more we will see ourselves and our circumstances grow in wholeness and completeness. That's because praise softens our hearts and makes them pliable.

STORMIE OMARTIAN
Praying God's Will for Your Life

ॐ

Because Your lovingkindness is
better than life, my lips shall praise You.
PSALM 63:3

Joy is the serious business of heaven. "There will more joy in heaven over one sinner who repents than over ninety-nine righteous persons who need no repentance." Jesus Christ has the last word. Not death. Not sin. Not anxiety. Not fear. The last word is joy.

HARRIET CROSBY
A Place Called Home

❧

There will more joy in heaven over one sinner who repents than over ninety-nine righteous persons who need no repentance.

LUKE 15:7

334

Jesus was tempted. The price of Satan's offers, on the face of it, was cheap—work a couple of small miracles, do obeisance to him. The price of obedience to the Father, on the other hand, was high. It would cost Him everything. Here was the real test of Jesus' trust, of His love for God, the purity of His purpose, the irrevocability of His commitment. He categorically refused every offer, meeting the test with the written Word.

ELISABETH ELLIOT
The Path of Loneliness

❦

*As the Father loved Me, I also
have loved you; abide in My love.*

JOHN 15:9

The relationship for which we were made, the relationship our heart never ceases to crave, is very specific. We are barely into the first chapter of the story when we encounter a significant fact: "Let *Us* make man in *Our* image." Making man was a relational affair from the very beginning. We were born in the womb of the greatest relationship the galaxies have ever known. God the Father, God the Son, and God the Holy Spirit. . . . God made us for Himself.

FAWN PARISH
It's All About You, Jesus

✥

He who loves Me will be loved by My Father.
JOHN 14:21

God is always revealing Himself to us through His Word and through the works of His hands. He's an intentional God, brimming over with purpose, infusing meaning into everything around us. But we need to open "the eyes of our heart."

JONI EARECKSON TADA
Holiness in Hidden Places

ॐ

*I ask . . . God . . . to make you intelligent
and discerning . . . to grasp the immensity
of this glorious way of life he has for Christians.*

EPHESIANS 1:17–18, *THE MESSAGE*

It's time to let God's love cover all things in your life. All secrets. All hurts. All hours of evil, minutes of worry.

Discover along with the psalmist: "He ... loads me with love and mercy." Picture a giant dump truck full of love. There you are behind it. God lifts the bed until the love starts to slide. Slowly at first, then down, down, down until you are hidden, buried, and covered in His love.

MAX LUCADO
A Love Worth Giving

༜

He ... loads me with love and mercy.
PSALM 103:4, NCV

God sees how our lives cross paths with others', both now and also around the bend, where we can't see. He places us in situations, not for our own benefit, but for the benefit of others. While we're stumbling around in the desert getting sand between our toes and whining like the Israelites, sometimes it helps to realize we have been placed where we are as the answer to someone else's prayers.

LESLIE WILLIAMS
Night Wrestling

❧

God is not unjust to forget your work
and labor of love....

HEBREWS 6:10

There are no trivial things in the Christian life.

If we yield ourselves to God each day and ask Him to guide us, we'll have the direction we need when we need it. If we don't, then we wait. God leads in little things and big things because He is making all things work together for good.

WARREN W. WIERSBE
The 20 Essential Qualities

ॐ

All things work together
for good to those who love God.

ROMANS 8:28

If we train ourselves, we can sense God's presence in every object or person we encounter during even a humdrum day; and recognizing the sparkle in the bubble is itself a way to worship the God who created bubbles and added sparkles just for the fun of it.

LESLIE WILLIAMS
Night Wrestling

*Great peace have those who love Your law,
and nothing causes them to stumble.*

PSALM 119:165

341

One day, when I get to my Father's House, all of my sins—my sinful thoughts, my sinful actions, my sinful attitudes—are going to fall away like a stinking garment that finally drops off and is discarded. What will be left will be the character of Christ that He has developed in me during my life on earth.

When I obeyed Him in the midst of suffering . . . when I chose to love instead of hate . . . *His character was being formed in me.*

ANNE GRAHAM LOTZ
Heaven

৵

Let this mind be in you
which was also in Christ Jesus.

PHILIPPIANS 2:5

Great wealth is not related to money. It is an attitude of satisfaction ("enough is enough") coupled with inner peace (an absence of churning) plus a day-by-day, moment-by-moment walk with God. . . .

In a word, the secret is *contentment*.

CHARLES SWINDOLL
Strengthening Your Grip

❧

My grace is sufficient for you.

2 CORINTHIANS 12:9

Sometimes the predictable, plannable future is exactly what we seek. If we plan carefully and thoroughly enough, then we think we will be secure. The problem with this attitude (I know it well) is that we have planned ourselves a flat future.

But worse that missing out on life's richest experiences is that we mistake the security of our plans for the security of God's love.

LESLIE WILLIAMS
Night Wrestling

&

*When I sit in darkness,
the LORD will be a light to me.*
MICAH 7:8

D id you know that you are God's
special loved one? Why would He
love you so? Maybe it's because when you
abide in Christ you are so saturated in Jesus
that when God looks at you, He sees His
own precious Son and envelopes you in His
love for Jesus' sake!

ANNE GRAHAM LOTZ
My Heart's Cry

⁓

If anyone loves Me, he will keep My word;
and My Father will love him.

JOHN 14:23

345

Did you notice the first five letters of the word *courteous* spell *court?* In old England, to be courteous was to act in the way of the court. The family and servants of the king were expected to follow a higher standard.

So are we. Are we not called to represent the King? Then "let your light shine before men, that they may see your good deeds and praise your Father in heaven."

MAX LUCADO
A Love Worth Giving

⌘

Let your light shine before men,
that they may see your good
deeds and praise your Father in heaven.

MATTHEW 5:16, NIV

God isn't interested in my image; He's concerned with my heart. Scripture tells me, "Man looks at the outward appearance, but the LORD looks at the heart" (1 Sam. 16:7). The choice of where to place my focus is mine.

LUCI SWINDOLL
I Married Adventure

ॐ

Man looks at the outward appearance,
but the LORD looks at the heart.

1 SAMUEL 16:7

Do you think God's silence in your life means He has forgotten you? Oh no! God says He has engraved your name on the palms of His hands. . . . You are in God's heart and on His mind every moment. He is fully informed of your circumstances and will bring about change when He knows the time is right.

ANNE GRAHAM LOTZ
God's Story

❧

*I have inscribed you
on the palms of My hands.*

ISAIAH 49:16

What we do for Jesus is vastly less important than who we *are* in Him. The crucial thing is to show up for duty daily, letting Him guide us into the ministry *He* needs accomplished—not the ministry we are on fire to accomplish on His behalf.

W. PHILLIP KELLER
Sea Edge

૪

God is able to make all grace abound toward you, that you . . . may have an abundance for every good work.

2 CORINTHIANS 9:8

Many times we make the mistake of thinking that Christ's help is needed only for sickrooms or in times of overwhelming sorrow and suffering. This is not true. Jesus wishes to enter into every mood and every moment of our lives. He went to the wedding at Cana as well as to the home of Mary and Martha when Lazarus died. He wept with those who wept and rejoiced with those who rejoiced.

BILLY GRAHAM
Unto the Hills

༈

Lo, I am with you always.
MATTHEW 28:20

Our self-fulfillment grows with discipline: the discipline of prayer, of love practiced on those who don't seem to notice, of doing our spiritual chores, of going to church, of reading the Bible, of repeatedly seeking the One who feeds us with the bread and water of life.

LESLIE WILLIAMS
Seduction of the Lesser Gods

❦

Reckon yourselves to be dead indeed to sin,
but alive to God in Christ Jesus our Lord.

ROMANS 6:11

351

When your dreams don't come true, you may be on the brink of learning to trust Jesus in a far deeper manner than you ever could have imagined. If all worked out well, you might put life on cruise control. What most enhances my relationship with Jesus is my ability to trust Him, no matter what the circumstances.

JOHN HULL AND TIM ELMORE
Pivotal Praying

ॐ

The LORD takes pleasure in . . .
those who hope in His mercy.
PSALM 147:11

B ecoming the person God longs for us to be doesn't happen easily or quickly. No one waves a magic wand over your head and—voila!—the Proverbs 31 woman emerges. It's a process of walking each day with Him. Giving Him permission to mold you, change you, shake you, move you. Little by little you will understand.

KATHY TROCCOLI
Hope for a Woman's Heart

He has made everything beautiful in its time.

ECCLESIASTES 3:11

353

When I meet a woman whose life is clearly filled with the fruit of kindness, I see a beautiful person regardless of her outward appearance. The kindness she shows to the world is really the Holy Spirit at work making the world a more beautiful place, showing forth the presence of God.

HARRIET CROSBY
A Well-Watered Garden

᧖

Let them shout for joy and be glad,
who favor my righteous cause.

PSALM 35:27

Our lives are like plotlines in a novel, with God as the Author. Nasty surprises or twists and turns of plot do not deter us from the path we tread. Because of the cross, we may march through earthly jungles, deserts, gardens, cities, but we are on a heavenly trek. No matter what our journeys lead us through, we always end up in God.

LESLIE WILLIAMS
Night Wrestling

3

Call upon Me in the day of trouble;
I will deliver you, and you shall glorify Me.
PSALM 50:15

When God made Sabbath holy, He made a statement of our utter dependency on Him. Sabbath is an assault on our mistaken notion that our striving, our haggling (either with man or God), our constant fervid expenditure of self-effort, is what we need to make our way in the world. Taking time off from the world and watching it still survive, tells us that the Lord is God, and we are not.

FAWN PARISH
It's All About You, Jesus

༁

The Son of Man is also Lord of the Sabbath.

MARK 2:28

Just as there was one door that led into God's presence in Eden and one door that led into the safety of the ark and one door that led into the inner sanctuary of the temple, a personal relationship with God is only accessed through one door—Jesus Himself.

ANNE GRAHAM LOTZ
My Heart's Cry

ॐ

I am the door.
If anyone enters by Me, he will be saved.

JOHN 10:9

357

We should all sleep like babies every night knowing we are children of the Lord, yet we look to stock portfolios, popularity, jobs, social standing, and other things to give us the security only God can give. We continually construct little emotional bomb shelters, ignoring the more profound gift God offers us, the deep sense that things are all right within us, that in Him we are safe at home.

W. PHILLIP KELLER
Sea Edge

∽

*Our help is in the name of the LORD,
who made heaven and earth.*

PSALM 124:8

Jesus reflects the perfect balance between knowing the truth and living from the heart. Jesus had neither a sterile, academic approach to life, nor an undue emphasis on emotionalism. He brings together our heads and our hearts to make us soulish persons who reflect the harmony of grace and truth, just as He did when He was on this earth. He gives us the will to walk according to His way.

LUCI SWINDOLL
I Married Adventure

෨

The law was given through Moses,
but grace and truth
came through Jesus Christ.
JOHN 1:17

God is our middle C.
A still point
in a turning world.
—Max Lucado

December 1

This month the birthday of Jesus Christ will be celebrated all over the world. It will be celebrated in various ways, in many languages, by people of all races. For a few hours many in the world will stop talking of satellites, rockets, and war. For a few hours they will talk of peace on earth and good will toward men. People will exchange their gifts and talk about the Prince of Peace.

BILLY GRAHAM
Unto the Hills

*His name will
be called . . .
Prince of Peace.*
ISAIAH 9:6

S in is similar to pollution. It is man-made through the power of choice. Unless dealt with aggressively, sin gathers, deepens, and obscures Truth. Only when we acknowledge sin for the pollution it really is can the clean-up effort begin.

God Himself stands ready to champion that clean-up effort. His assistance arrives the very moment we move from denial to repentance.

ALICIA BRITT CHOLE
Pure Joy

∽

*If we confess our sins, He is faithful
and just to forgive us our sins
and to cleanse us from all unrighteousness.*

1 JOHN 1:9

Dawn follows darkness. Sunset follows day. Our short sojourn here is marked off in the steady rhythm of the seasons, tides, moons and sunsets. Each is a beautiful reminder—"O my Father, You are nigh! Your glory fills the whole earth! All is well with my soul! In Your presence there is joy forevermore!"

W. PHILLIP KELLER
Sea Edge

༈

Let the hearts of those
rejoice who seek the LORD!
PSALM 105:3

I love the fact that God has a plan for the future, for every tomorrow of my life on earth and beyond. Even though I can't figure it all out, He's got it wired. This reassures me that I'm loved and safe.

LUCI SWINDOLL
I Married Adventure

I know the plans I have for you, . . .
plans to prosper you and not to harm you.

JEREMIAH 29:11, NIV

Christ died not just for my blatant sins, but for the subtle ones as well: for all my mixed motives, for the acts of kindness that wound others inadvertently, for self-doubt, for the desire to think well of myself. Christ redeems me every time I open my mouth, and He redeems every gesture I make toward goodness—or evil.

I am clean because I have been washed in the blood of the Lamb of God.

LESLIE WILLIAMS
Seduction of the Lesser Gods

෪

My lips shall greatly rejoice
when I sing to You,
and my soul, which You have redeemed.

PSALM 71:23

If it's any encouragement to you, there isn't a praying person anywhere who hasn't felt the pain of waiting on answered prayer. It's part of the package of being a follower of Jesus. If all the answers came overnight, we would not be called a people of faith.

JOHN HULL AND TIM ELMORE
Pivotal Praying

*I prayed, and the LORD has granted me
my petition which I asked of Him.*
1 SAMUEL 1:27

367

We are not our possessions, but our material things reveal where our hearts lie. Serious Christians need to consider what we are saying with our toys. No wonder Francis of Assisi dropped his inheritance (and his clothes) in the middle of the square and walked into his new life buck naked. Having no possessions at all certainly simplified his life. For those of us who cannot give everything away, the sorting of belongings is a prayerful task.

LESLIE WILLIAMS
Night Wrestling

⋑

*If riches increase,
do not set your heart on them.*

PSALM 62:10

I want a reason to get up in the morning. When I ask God for a sense of personal destiny, and then listen carefully, I get a sense of direction. Not always, and not always immediately, but I rely on God's promises to consistently guide me toward fulfilling the purpose for which He created me.

LUCI SWINDOLL
I Married Adventure

ꝏ

In his heart a man plans his course,
but the LORD determines his steps.
PROVERBS 16:9, NIV

How wonderful it is that God calls the seemingly unqualified to serve Him. Few of us are the eldest, the brightest, the most beautiful, or the most gifted. But God does not judge us by our outward appearance.

God places His hand upon the urban and rural, simple and sophisticated, trendy and traditional, country and country club, hip and hick,…and turns shepherds into kings.

ALICIA BRITT CHOLE
Pure Joy

☙

Man looks at the outward appearance,
but the LORD looks at the heart.

1 SAMUEL 16:7

Circumstances occur that could easily crush us. They may originate on the job or at home or even during the weekend when we are relaxing. Unexpectedly, they come. Immediately we have a choice to make …an attitude choice. We can hand the circumstances to God and ask Him to take control or we can roll up our mental sleeves and slug it out. Joy awaits our decision.

CHARLES SWINDOLL
Strengthening Your Grip

*Whoever is wise will …
understand the
lovingkindness of the LORD.*
PSALM 107:43

I sn't it amazing how pain and pressure and problems can so totally preoccupy our attention that they make even the best of us completely self-centered? If someone suggested to you that you help another person in need, would you respond harshly with a scowling face, "I couldn't possibly. You have no idea what I'm going through myself"? Like me, you may need reminding that serving Jesus by serving others when it's not convenient to do so is one secret to overcoming the pain and pressures in our own lives.

ANNE GRAHAM LOTZ
My Heart's Cry

ॐ

*Through love,
serve one another.*
GALATIANS 5:13

Every person is a combination of many factors woven together from the joys and sorrows of life. We're also the product of our choices. We're the result of what was or was not done for us or to us by our parents, siblings, associates, and friends. The journey we're on is planned and watched over by a loving God who wants us to treasure the gift of being alive and who sets us free to participate in our own destiny.

LUCI SWINDOLL
I Married Adventure

⌘

Behold, I am the LORD, the God of all flesh.
Is there anything too hard for Me?
JEREMIAH 32:27

The Lord is not confined to the pages of Holy Writ. He is not to be found only in our solemn sanctuaries. He is not restricted to liturgy or creed.

He is everywhere at work in our weary old world. He is to be met in a thousand disguises. His touch is to be found at every turn of the trail.

W. PHILLIP KELLER
Sea Edge

༄

The LORD is your shade at your right hand.
PSALM 121:5

Jesus humbled himself. He went from commanding angels to sleeping in the straw. From holding stars to clutching Mary's finger. The palm that held the universe took the nail of a soldier.

Why? Because that's what love does. It puts the beloved before itself.

MAX LUCADO
A Love Worth Giving

By this we know love, because He
laid down His life for us.
1 JOHN 3:16

375

God's Word has been preserved, not merely as a collection of historical documents and geographical studies, but as a trustworthy resource—a place we turn to for assistance in living our lives in ways that honor Christ.

In the pages of Scripture, God has given us models—people, believe it or not, who are just like you and me, who, despite the odds, lived lives pleasing to Him. By faith. In obedience. With courage.

CHARLES SWINDOLL
Paul: A Man of Grace and Grit

✃

My soul keeps Your testimonies,
and I love them exceedingly.

PSALM 119:167

God is our future. We don't need to worry about our maps, our timetables, our plans, because if we are on the spiritual journey, we have already reached our goal— to live and be in Christ.

LESLIE WILLIAMS
Night Wrestling

&

All the paths of the LORD are mercy and truth, to such as keep His covenant.

PSALM 25:10

Humble, ordinary things can be very holy, very full of God....

While angels were singing for the shepherds, [Mary] was sweating and straining in the darkness and discomfort of a stable.... Her mind could hardly have been filled with pure exulting. It was a *baby*, a human baby, helpless and squalling, that she must attend to. She was the "handmaid of the Lord," carrying out her task in pain and squalor, neither seeing (so far as we know) the glory of the Lord nor hearing the angels' song.

ELISABETH ELLIOT
The Music of His Promises

༄

I'm the Lord's maid, ready to serve.
LUKE 1:38, *THE MESSAGE*

Many of us would like to avoid the mills of God. We are tempted to ask Him to deliver us from the upsetting, tumbling tides of time that knock off our rough corners and shape us to His design. We plead for release from the discipline of difficulties, the rub of responsibilities, the polish that comes from perseverance.

But God's ways and our ways are not the same. His patience is persistent. His work is meticulous.

W. PHILLIP KELLER
Sea Edge

ॐ

You are my God, I will exalt You.
PSALM 118:28

K ind hearts are quietly kind. They let the car cut into traffic and the young mom with three kids move up in the checkout line. They pick up the neighbor's trash can that rolled into the street. And they are especially kind at church. They understand that perhaps the neediest person they'll meet all week is the one standing in the foyer or sitting on the row behind them in worship.

MAX LUCADO
A Love Worth Giving

꒛

When we have the opportunity
to help anyone, we should do it. But we should
give special attention
to those who are in the family of believers.
GALATIANS 6:10, NCV

There are hours when your heart is filled with love and praise, and you're quite sure this feeling will last forever. But it doesn't, because every summit introduces a valley. The test of our devotion to Christ isn't our occasional triumphing on the mountain so much as our patient trudging on the plain and courageous struggling through the valley.

WARREN W. WIERSBE
The 20 Essential Qualities

ॐ

My heart is steadfast,
O God, …
I will sing and give praise.
PSALM 57:7

381

December 21

From the cradle in Bethlehem to the cross in Jerusalem we've pondered the love of our Father. What can you say to that kind of emotion? Upon learning that God would rather die than live without you, how do you react? How can you begin to explain such passion?

MAX LUCADO
In the Grip of Grace

That you . . . may . . . know . . .
the love of Christ which passes knowledge.
EPHESIANS 3:17–19

The goal is spiritual balance—an impossible feat to manage unless we continually tend the inner garden [of our hearts] with prayer, tossing distractions back over the wall as they invade our privacy. If we scurry about, doing God's work without time for reflection, then we get out of sorts with ourselves, our children, and other people.

The great temptation is to think that an unbalanced life is not a serious problem. Big mistake.

LESLIE WILLIAMS
Night Wrestling

꒳

It is no longer I who live,
but Christ lives in me.
GALATIANS 2:20

December 23

Togetherness flourishes at Christmastime. During this one brief season each year our frustrated, old, world almost achieves the Kingdom of God on earth. For the term *kingdom of God* really means "kingdom of right relationships," and this is specifically what the Christ child came to earth to make possible.

CATHERINE MARSHALL
Moments that Matter

❧

Glory to God in the highest,
and on earth peace, goodwill toward men!

LUKE 2:14

The careless hand of man, the cruel ways of our society, the thoughtless acts and omitted courtesies of my contemporaries leave a legacy of hurts and sorrow and wreckage in my life.

Only Christ can change all this. Only He can alter the contours of my disposition. Only He can displace the debris of my soul with the surging newness of His own person.

W. PHILLIP KELLER
Sea Edge

ॐ

Restore us,
O God of our salvation.
PSALM 85:4

Christmas is not just an annual holiday. It is not a day to glorify selfishness and materialism. Christmas is the celebration of the event that set heaven to singing, an event that gave the stars of the night sky a new brilliance.

Christmas tells us that at a specific time and at a specific place a specific Person was born: "God of God, Light of Light, very God of very God"—the Lord, Jesus Christ.

BILLY GRAHAM
Unto the Hills

✥

I have come that they may have life,
and have it more abundantly.

JOHN 10:10

Decisions and choices. Choices and decisions. We make thousands of them every day. Clearly, we are a people in great need of direction. Maybe we need a sign. Maybe we need someone to tell us what to do and where we should go.

And then there's prayer.

JOHN HULL AND TIM ELMORE
Pivotal Praying

Pray without ceasing.
1 THESSALONIANS 5:17

I f Jesus were on TV today advertising what He has to offer, what would a commercial for the ideal spiritual life be like? According to Luke 6, Jesus promotes the following characteristics: poverty, hunger, weeping, being hated. Matthew 5 continues the list: mourning, meekness, mercy, pureness in heart, peacemaking, being persecuted.

Can you imagine how an ad for these qualities would run? What Jesus wants for us is *not* the American dream.

LESLIE WILLIAMS
Night Wrestling

᠕

Blessed are the meek,
for they shall inherit the earth.

MATTHEW 5:5

Joy is a choice. It is a matter of attitude that stems from one's confidence in God— that He is at work, that He is in full control, that He is in the midst of whatever has happened, is happening, and will happen.

CHARLES SWINDOLL
Laugh Again

~

*Let Your priests be clothed
with righteousness, and
let Your saints shout for joy.*
PSALM 132:9

389

The Bible is an amazing volume of work—like no other! In sixty-six books there is perfect historical continuity from the creation of the world to the new heaven and the new earth. Truths constantly unfold, prophecy is fulfilled, and the most perfect Person on earth or in heaven is anticipated, presented, realized, and exalted. . . . The book is a phenomenon.

LUCI SWINDOLL
I Married Adventure

෨

The entrance
of Your words gives light;
it gives understanding.
PSALM 119:130

I n the Old Testament, the glory of God
appeared to the Children of Israel as a pillar
of cloud by day and a pillar of fire by night....

But the Bible says God's glory is no longer
revealed in a cloudy, fiery pillar [or] a golden,
glowing cloud. . . . The glory of God is within
you and me through the Spirit of God. You
and I are the display cases for God's glory as
His living temples.

ANNE GRAHAM LOTZ
God's Story

~

*Do you not know that you
are the temple of God,
and that the Spirit of God dwells in you?*
1 CORINTHIANS 3:16

December 31

Life in all its definitions is a gift from God. We do not create ourselves. We cannot force the earth to sustain us for one extra day outside the will of God. Life is technically a heartbeat, a brainwave; life is also a communion for eternity with the one God of the universe. We choose it best when we give it back to the One who gave it to us in the first place.

LESLIE WILLIAMS
Seduction of the Lesser Gods

❧

Of Him you are in Christ Jesus,
who became for us wisdom from God.
1 CORINTHIANS 1:30

Acknowledgments

Grateful acknowledgment is made to the following publishers for permission to reprint this copyrighted material.

Bevere, Lisa. *Be Angry but Don't Blow it!* (Nashville, Thomas Nelson, 2000)

———— *Kissed the Girls and Made Them Cry,* (Nashville: Thomas Nelson Publishers, 2002).

Brestin, Dee and Kathy Troccoli. *The Colors of His Love,* (Nashville: W Publishing, 2002).

Chole, Alicia Britt. *Pure Joy,* (Nashville: J. Countryman, 2003).

Crosby, Harriet. *A Well-Watered Garden,* (Nashville: Thomas Nelson, Inc., 1995).

————*A Place Called Home,* (Nashville: Thomas Nelson Publishers, 1997).

Elliot, Elisabeth. *The Path of Loneliness,* (Nashville: Thomas Nelson Publishers, 1988).

————*The Music of His Promises: Listening to God with Love, Trust, and Obedience,* (Ann Arbor: Servant Publications, 2000)

Ezell, Suzanne Dale. *Living Again in God's Abundance,* (Nashville: Thomas Nelson, Inc., 2002)

Graham, Billy. *Unto the Hills: A Daily Devotional* (Nashville: W Publishing, 1996).

————*The Secret of Happiness,* (Nashville: W Publishing, 2002).

Hawthorne, Steve S. *Perspectives On the World Christian Movement,* (Pasadena: William Carey Library, 1993).

Hull, John and Tim Elmore. *Pivotal Praying,* (Nashville: Thomas Nelson Publishers, 2002).

Johnson, Barbara. *He's Gonna Toot and I'm Gonna Scoot,* (Nashville: W Publishing, 1999).

—————*Leaking Laffs Between Pampers and Depends*, (Nashville: W Publishing, 2000).

Keller, W. Phillip. *Sea Edge*, (Nashville: W Publishing, 1985).

Lotz, Anne Graham. *God's Story*, (Nashville: W Publishing, 1997).

—————*Heaven: My Father's House*, (Nashville: W Publishing, 2001).

—————*My Heart's Cry*, (Nashville: W Publishing, 2002).

Lucado, Max. *The Applause of Heaven* (Nashville: W. Publishing Group, 1990).

—————*In the Eye of the Storm* (Nashville: W. Publishing Group, 1991).

—————*He Still Moves Stones* (Nashville: W. Publishing Group, 1993).

—————*When God Whispers Your Name* (Nashville: W. Publishing Group, 1994).

—————*In the Grip of Grace* (Nashville: W. Publishing Group, 1996).

—————*The Great House of God* (Nashville: W. Publishing Group , 1997).

—————*Just Like Jesus* (Nashville: W. Publishing Group, 1998).

—————*When Christ Comes* (Nashville: W. Publishing Group, 1999).

—————*Traveling Light* (Nashville: W. Publishing Group, 2001).

—————*A Love Worth Giving*, (Nashville: W Publishing, 2002).

Marshall, Catherine. *Moments that Matter*, (Nashville: J Countryman, 2001).

Omartian, Stormie. *Praying God's Will for Your Life*, (Nashville: Thomas Nelson Publishers, 2001).

Parish, Fawn. *It's All About You, Jesus*, (Nashville: Thomas Nelson Publishers, 2001).

Smedes, Lewis. *Keeping Hope Alive*, (Nashville: Thomas Nelson Publishers, 1998).

Swindoll, Charles. *Living Above the Level of Mediocrity*, (Nashville: W. Publishing Group, 1981).

—————*Strengthening Your Grip*, (Nashville: W. Publishing Group, 1982).

—————*Dropping Your Guard*, (Nashville: W. Publishing Group, 1983).

—————*The Finishing Touch*, (Nashville: W. Publishing Group, 1994).

—————*Laugh Again*, (Nashville: W. Publishing Group, 1994).

—————*The Mystery of God's Will*, (Nashville: W. Publishing Group, 1995).

—————*Moses: A Man of Selfless Dedication*, (Nashville: W. Publishing Group, 1999).

—————*Perfect Trust*, (Nashville: J. Countryman, 2000).

————*Day by Day with Charles Swindoll,* (Nashville: W. Publishing Group, 2000).

————*Paul: A Man of Grace and Grit,* (Nashville: W. Publishing Group, 2002).

Swindoll, Luci. *I Married Adventure,* (Nashville: W Publishing, 2002).

Tada, Joni Eareckson. *Holiness in Hidden Places,* (Nashville: J. Countryman, 1999).

Trobisch, Ingrid. *The Confident Woman,* (Bolivar, MO: Quiet Waters Publications, 2001) www.quietwaterspub.com.

Troccoli, Kathy. *Hope for a Woman's Heart,* (Nashville: J. Countryman, 2002).

Thomas, Angela. *Do You Think I'm Beautiful?* (Nashville: Thomas Nelson Publishers, 2003).

Wallace, Peter. *What the Psalmist Is Saying* (Nashville: Thomas Nelson, 1995).

Wiersbe, Warren W. *The 20 Essential Qualities of an Authentic Christian,* (Nashville: Thomas Nelson Publishers, 1996).

Williams, Leslie. *Night Wrestling: Struggling for Answers and Finding God,* (Nashville: W Publishing, 1997).

————*Seduction of the Lesser Gods,* (Nashville: W Publishing, 1997).